D0616692

The Fall and Rise of the Pentagon

Recent Titles in
Contributions in Political Science
Series Editor: Bernard K. Johnpoll

The Fall and Rise of the Pentagon

AMERICAN DEFENSE POLICIES IN THE 1970s

Lawrence J. Korb

Contributions in Political Science, Number 27

GREENWOOD PRESS
WESTPORT, CONNECTICUT • LONDON, ENGLAND

355.0213
K84f

Library of Congress Cataloging in Publication Data

Korb, Lawrence J   1939-
  The fall and rise of the Pentagon.

  (Contributions in political science; no. 27
ISSN 0147-1066)
  Bibliography: p.
  Includes index.
    1. United States.   Dept. of Defense—History.
2. United States—Military policy.   3. United States—
Politics and government—1945-   I. Title.
II. Series.
UA23.6.K67   355.02'13'0973   78-73795
ISBN 0-313-21087-X

Library of Congress Catalog Card Number: 78-73795
ISBN: 0-313-21087-X
ISSN: 0147-1066

First published in 1979

Greenwood Press, Inc.
51 Riverside Avenue, Westport, Connecticut 06880

Printed in the United States of America

10 9 8 7 6 5 4 3 2

205561

To Ann
My Helper and Inspiration

Contents

Tables

Illustrations

Preface

While it may be overstating the case to argue that the national defense establishment was near collapse at the close of the 1960s, there is no doubt that the United States military was in serious difficulty. The Pentagon had very little external support; internally, it was dispirited. Yet within a decade, the situation was almost reversed. One indication of the Pentagon's rise was public reaction to President Carter's first defense budget. In January 1978 when the Chief Executive, who campaigned on a platform of reduced defense expenditures, proposed to increase the defense budget by only $10 billion or 8 percent, he was roundly denounced by most legislators and by many members of the foreign policy elite for his lack of support for the military. Congress, under intense pressure from its constituents and the armed services, added funds to the President's proposed defense program for the fiscal year (FY) 1979, something it had not done for fifteen years.

This book will trace the decline of the Pentagon, analyze how and why the world's largest bureaucracy coped with the hostile environment, and outline the turnaround or rise in the fortunes of the military establishment. Although the domestic and international environment played a significant part in the fall and rise of the Pentagon, this study will show that the actions of the civilian and military leaders of the Department of Defense were the crucial variable in both cases.

Much of the data upon which this analysis is based comes from open literature. However, many of the perspectives offered were gained when I interviewed and worked with members of the defense hierarchy as a consultant during the 1970s. Although one hopes that scholarly objectivity is never compromised, the reader should be forewarned that I have been extensively involved with both civilian and military leaders of the national security bureaucracy since 1972.

Acknowledgments

The production of any book normally involves the direct and indirect assistance and inspiration of many people. This work is no exception. Although it is not feasible to thank everyone individually, I would like to pay special tribute to three groups who provided aid and encouragement: those overworked civil servants in the Department of Defense and the Office of Management and Budget who took time from their too busy schedules to discuss defense issues with a neophyte from outside the government; the staff of the American Enterprise Institute for Public Policy Research who some years ago gave a then young scholar the opportunity to investigate and analyze defense budgetary questions; and the staff, students, and faculty at the Naval War College who over the past four years have stimulated my interest in and challenged my assumptions about defense policy. Although none of these individuals bears any responsibility for what follows in this book, each and every one of them has influenced its content.   Lawrence J. Korb

The Fall and Rise
of the Pentagon

CHAPTER 1

The Decline
of the Military

Introduction

The Allied military victory over the Axis powers in Europe and Asia was made possible by material and men furnished by the United States. This nation provided well over $100 billion worth of supplies and equipment to its allies and threw some 12 million people into the battle against Germany and Japan. In addition, it was primarily United States military leadership that directed the Allied effort in this worldwide conflict. The invasion of Normandy and the drive to the Elbe were coordinated by General Dwight D. Eisenhower, while the island-hopping campaigns in the Pacific were directed by General Douglas MacArthur and Admiral Chester Nimitz. American flag officers also directed most of the subordinate military commands. General Omar Bradley commanded 1.3 million soldiers in the march across Europe and Admiral William Halsey led the carrier task forces which invaded those remote Pacific islands which served as stepping stones to the Japanese homeland. The United States and the rest of the world thrilled to the exploits of "blood and guts" Patton in North Africa and Europe and "31 knot" Burke in the Pacific.

This colossal victory of our forces in World War II not only gave the United States its highest prestige in history, but also enhanced the power of the armed forces within our society. Although the United States began to demobilize briefly after the cessation of hostilities following World War II, the outbreak of the Cold War and the Communist attack against South Korea dramatically reversed that process and this nation once again turned to its military leaders. General MacArthur was dispatched from Japan to take charge of the United Nations' response to the attack on South Korea. General Eisenhower was recalled to active duty from the presidency of Columbia University and sent back to Europe to establish the military arm of the North Atlantic Treaty Organization (NATO). General Bradley was moved from the Veterans Administration to become the first Chairman of the newly created Joint Chiefs of Staff (JCS)—a permanent military committee established to provide military advice to the President, the National Security Council, the Secretary of Defense, and the Congress.

The Privileged Position: 1950-1968

From the outbreak of the Korean War in June 1950 through the TET offensive in January 1968, the American military enjoyed a privileged position within the American political system.[1] During most of this period the leaders and the people of the United States felt that they were involved in a global struggle against world communism. Consequently, for the first time in its history, this nation established a large, permanent, standing military force composed of several million people. As indicated in Table 1, prior to the post-World War II period the size of the United States regular army never

Table 1   Army Size, 1800-1939

	Regular Army Average Size	Percentage of National Population
1800-1809	3,666	0.069
1810-1819	14,433	0.199
1820-1829	6,359	0.066
1830-1839	8,167	0.063
1840-1849	19,157	0.112
1850-1859	13,695	0.059
1860-1869	393,255	1.251
1870-1879	28,297	0.071
1880-1889	26,495	0.053
1890-1899	51,050	0.081
1900-1909	77,108	0.101
1910-1919	433,266	0.471
1920-1929	154,171	0.146
1930-1939	155,246	0.126

"Average size" for a decade is arrived at by averaging the regular army force levels for each year of the decade. The population data is for the first year of each decade.

Source: James Clotfelter, *The Military in American Politics* (New York: Harper and Row, 1973), p. 14.

exceeded one-tenth of 1 percent of the national population in a non-shooting war situation. Before World War II this nation's army was the sixteenth largest in the world, putting it behind such small nations as Yugoslavia, Turkey, Spain, Romania, and Poland.

After 1950, however, the newly created Department of Defense (DOD) was given access to whatever manpower resources it needed via the selective service system. Moreover, since those who were drafted or who volunteered because induction was imminent received only subsistence wages, the Pentagon received its manpower at virtually no cost. The average pay of recruits throughout most of the 1950-1968 period was only $78 a month.

From 1950 through 1968, defense spending, even with its low-cost manpower, accounted for more than half of the total federal budget and consumed approximately 10 percent of this nation's gross national product (GNP).[2] At the beginning of 1968, the Pentagon had 3.5 million military men and 1.3 million civilians on its payroll and 1.6 million men in the reserve and national guard. The DOD operated several thousand bases in this country and over five hundred military installations abroad. Approximately 1.2 million men were stationed in thirty foreign countries, and the United States was committed to the defense of forty-three other nations. In its inventory, the United States had 1,710 strategic missiles, 650 intercontinental bombers, 5,700 tactical aircraft, 350 major combatant surface ships, and about 100 attack submarines. The total value of the Pentagon's assets exceeded $500 billion.

During the 1950-1968 period, within the councils of government the Pentagon and its leaders had a strong impact on policy. General Bradley, as Chairman of the Joint Chiefs of Staff (JCS), ranked with Dean Acheson as one of Truman's closest and most trusted advisers. His successor, Admiral Arthur Radford, was held in extremely high regard by President Eisenhower, and General Maxwell Taylor was a confidant of both John Kennedy and Lyndon Johnson. On the middle-management level, the well organized and well disciplined military planners usually dominated their civilian counterparts in the State Department and other civilian agencies of the national security bureaucracy. Military influence was not confined to those on active duty. Many retired career officers occupied high-level positions throughout the federal government. General Eisenhower served as

President for eight years. His mentor, General George Marshall, held the two most prestigious positions in the cabinet. Marshall served as both Secretary of State and Secretary of Defense in the Truman administration. Admiral William Raborn and Walter Bedell Smith and Hoyt Vandenberg, both generals, headed the CIA while Admiral Lewis Strauss directed the Atomic Energy Commission. General Bradley was the first director of the Veterans Administration. In addition, several retired career officers served as ambassadors to key nations. General Taylor was ambassador to South Vietnam in the Johnson administration, General Walter B. Smith was ambassador to the Soviet Union under Eisenhower, and President Kennedy made General James Gavin U.S. envoy to France and Admiral George Anderson the head of the U.S. mission in Portugal.[3] The DOD also had strong support from Congress. The legislative branch always treated the Pentagon budget more kindly than the non-defense portions of the federal budget. Moreover, at the urging of the JCS, Congress frequently pressured the President to build more sophisticated and more numerous weapon systems. It was the Congress that initially prodded the executive to be more sympathetic to military requests for manned bombers, nuclear-powered ships, intercontinental ballistic missiles, submarine-launched ballistic missiles, and the antiballistic missile system (ABM).

The military enjoyed widespread support from the American public as well. Despite the large portion of the federal budget allocated to defense spending, the percentage of those favoring a reduction in defense spending between 1950 and 1968 was never more than 10 percent. Moreover, during the same period, close to 30 percent of the people actually favored an increase in defense outlays. The remaining 60 percent generally supported the existing high level of defense spending.[4] Public support manifested itself in several other ways. The military consistently ranked among the most admired institutions in American society. Most parents considered a military career highly desirable for their male offspring. The three service academies were deluged with applications and congressional appointments to West Point, Annapolis, and Colorado Springs were powerful sources of political patronage.[5]

By the mid-1960s, the United States was the world's preeminent power and most of that preeminence was a result of its military strength. Reputable scholars such as Raymond Aron and George

Liska were speaking of American hegemony.[6] The Soviets had backed down in the Cuban missile crisis when confronted by overwhelming American nuclear and conventional forces. The Pentagon claimed that it had sufficient forces to fight two major and one minor or brush fire war simultaneously. The United States had strong capabilities across the entire spectrum of military power. Its Secretary of Defense could boast that this nation could afford to spend whatever was necessary on national defense;[7] Senator Gaylord Nelson (D-Wis.) could proclaim that the two most important words in the American vocabulary were "national defense." When the Vietnam War began in earnest in 1965, the Pentagon was able to put about a million men into the Southeast Asia theater without calling up the reserves or reducing its strength or commitments in other parts of the globe. The DOD poured almost $200 billion into the war on communism in Southeast Asia while other government agencies vigorously pursued the "War on Poverty" at home. For a while it appeared that this nation could have both guns and butter without a tax increase.

Blunders in Vietnam

The simultaneous attacks by the North Vietnamese and Vietcong on major cities and towns during the Tet holidays in early 1968 marked the end of this "era of good feeling" for the American military. No longer would it enjoy the same privileged position in the American political system. The Tet attacks themselves did not change the environment within which DOD had existed for nearly two decades. However, the actions of the North Vietnamese and the Vietcong forced the civilian leadership and the American public to face up to the reality of the situation in Vietnam, that is, that the United States, despite its overwhelming military force, did not possess the power to achieve its goal of an independent, viable South Vietnam. Moreover, in facing the reality of the situation in Vietnam, many people began to question the whole thrust of our post-World War II foreign policy and the impact of military considerations in the formulation and implementation of that policy.

In many ways the Tet offensive was like opening Pandora's box. Soon after the attacks, the work of such revisionist historians as Harry Magdoff and Gabriel Kolko gained new credence.[8] It now seemed plausible to many that if the United States could pursue such an absurd policy in Vietnam, perhaps the whole Cold War had resulted from a similarly absurd American foreign policy. Concern about the military industrial complex which had been dormant since Eisenhower's farewell address began to be expressed anew. Even military leaders began to wonder about the effects of the military on American society. General David Shoup, Medal of Honor winner in the Battle of Tarawa in 1943 and Commandant of the Marine Corps and a member of the JCS from 1959 through 1963, wrote in early 1969 that America had become a militaristic and aggressive nation and that militarism in America was in full bloom and promised a future of vigorous self-pollination, unless the blight of Vietnam revealed that militarism was more a poisonous weed than a glamorous blossom.[9]

The soul-searching that followed in the wake of the Tet offensive also brought to light many problems within the military. General Westmoreland, the commanding general of American forces in Vietnam, who had been *Time* magazine's "man of the year" in 1967, and who had been the first active duty military officer to address a joint session of the Congress, was relieved soon after Tet. Close analysis revealed that his battlefield tactics in Vietnam were disastrous. It appeared that Westmoreland had misperceived the situation in Vietnam completely. He had sought to conquer territory in a war that involved control of the population; he had employed battalion-sized units in operations that called for squads.[10] Moreover, the "inevitable general"[11] seemed unaware of or insensitive to the race and drug problems among our troops. Many military historians felt that Westmoreland was the worst American battlefield leader since George McLellan, a general who had to be relieved by Lincoln during the early part of the Civil War.

Ethical Aberrations

Not only was the judgment of American military leadership suspect as a result of Vietnam, but its integrity suffered as well. General John Lavelle, commander of the Seventh Air Force in Vietnam, had his subordinates write false reports to conceal the fact that he was conducting unauthorized air strikes against North Vietnam. In his defense, Lavelle claimed that he was prompted to take this action by a representative of the JCS.[12] When Lavelle's conduct was brought to light by an enlisted man, public confidence was further eroded when he was not prosecuted but allowed to retire on a $27,000 annual pension.

The JCS itself became involved in a secret bombing campaign against Communist forces in Cambodia. At the instigation of President Nixon, the Chiefs devised a dual reporting system which kept knowledge of the operations from all but a handful of people. This resulted in the Secretary of the Air Force and the Air Force Vice Chief of Staff inadvertently misleading Congress.

In many cases, the quality of leadership below the top echelons was also poor. Many military commanders showed more concern with careerism than with making a contribution to the situation in Southeast Asia. Ticket-punching and good fitness reports appeared to take priority over concrete results. Reports on combat activity were fabricated to impress senior commanders. Military decorations were awarded for innocuous missions. One high-ranking officer ordered his subordinates to recommend him for a Silver Star. Some officers showed more concern with outdoing their sister services in meeting contrived efficiency measures than with defeating the enemy.[13] The Navy and Air Force competed with each other to see who could drop more tonnage on North Vietnam. Some Army and Marine units engaged in a body count sweepstakes in South Vietnam. These contests resulted in inflated bombing statistics, exaggerated body counts, and misleading predictions about the "light at the end of the tunnel."[14]

As a result of this poor leadership and because of the frustrations of fighting in an almost impossible situation, morale suffered drastically. Race and drug problems were rampant. As early as 1965, about 32 percent of the troops in Vietnam were using illicit drugs. By the end of the decade the figures had increased to 50 percent. Of that number, more than half had used heroin. Some enlisted men attempted to destroy weapon systems, refused to go on combat missions, and even tried to kill senior officers and noncommissioned officers by fragging (attempting to murder a fellow serviceman with a fragmentation grenade). Fragging incidents rose to over three hundred annually by the end of the decade. Other enlisted men simply deserted their units. Desertion rates for the armed services rose from 13.2 per thousand in 1967 to over 30 per thousand by the end of the decade. Rates of desertion were highest among Army personnel who bore the brunt of the fighting in Vietnam. By the close of the 1960s, more than 73 out of every 1,000 soldiers were deserting.[15]

However, the events that really shocked the nation were the atrocities committed by American troops in Vietnam. The most publicized of these incidents occurred at My Lai where at least 175 and possibly more than 400 Vietnamese civilians were murdered by American soldiers in March 1968. In addition, at My Lai the American troops also committed individual and group acts of rape, sodomy, maiming, and assault on noncombatants and burned their dwellings.

The report on this incident, completed by General William Peers, named thirty individuals who by admission or commission showed culpability for trying to cover up the event.[16] Eventually, sixteen men were charged, but only four went to trial and only one, Lieutenant William Calley, was convicted. The fact that the only man convicted was a junior officer with a reserve commission only compounded the My Lai problem. In the minds of many, the military establishment appeared to be making a non-career reservist the scapegoat for the entire affair.

The Decline of the Pentagon

The American military leaders did not immediately recognize the significance of the Tet offensive. The JCS looked upon the Tet attacks as an opportunity to deliver a knockout blow to the Communists and urged President Johnson to send 200,000 additional troops to Vietnam to achieve a military victory. When the President, at the insistence of Secretary of Defense Clark Clifford, turned down their request, the Chiefs were shocked, and many military leaders adopted a "stab in the back" posture, that is, they could have won the war but were not permitted to do so by the civilian leaders.[17]

Despite the fact that the Pentagon hierarchy did not recognize it immediately, a new era had dawned for the American military. No longer would DOD be able to turn the manpower spigot on at will and receive a fresh supply of virtually free manpower. No longer would military leaders be revered as conquering heroes and welcomed into the councils of government. Eisenhower, the commanding general in Europe in World War II, could be elected President easily on two occasions, but the commanding general in Vietnam, William Westmoreland, could not even win the Republican primary for governor of South Carolina, nor was he given any high-level presidential appointment.[18] No longer would Congress perfunctorily pass multibillion dollar defense budgets. No longer would the American people willingly send their sons into the military and enthusiastically support high levels of defense spending. In a survey conducted by the Chicago Council on Foreign Relations only 14 percent of the American people favored the use of the military to aid South Korea if that nation were attacked by North Korea. Almost 70 percent of those surveyed opposed American involvement on the Korean peninsula.[19] Moreover, by 1970 a majority of the American public favored a reduction in defense spending![20]

Many of the myths that had sustained the military and brought public support had been destroyed in Vietnam. The Marines assaulted as many beaches in Vietnam as they did in World War II, but instead of entrenched Japanese soldiers, they were greeted by giggling Vietnamese schoolgirls. The Army's elite 101st Air Cavalry Unit did not drop any paratroopers into Vietnam as they had done in Normandy. Instead, "The Big Red One" became just another helicopter unit, searching for an elusive peasant army in elephant grass. The Navy's nuclear-powered aircraft carrier *Enterprise* sent its sophisticated jet aircraft to bomb footbridges and fishing junks rather than military targets in the Soviet Union. The B-52 bombers of the Air Force's Strategic Air Command carpet bombed dense jungles in South Vietnam rather than destroying the population and industry of the Communist world. Moreover, a large portion of the battlefield exploits of the American fighting men were drowned in a sea of actual and alleged atrocities. Many observers noted poignantly that in the early 1960s the United States placed the military in Vietnam to save that nation, but by the late 1960s our forces had to be taken out in order to save the military.[21]

Turmoil within the Pentagon

Vietnam was not the only source of problems for the American military in the late 1960s. Robert McNamara, whose seven-year tenure as Secretary of Defense had ended simultaneously with the

Tet attacks, had instituted a system of decision making in the Pentagon that had not only virtually excluded the military from the defense policy process but had denigrated the contribution that military experience and intuition might be capable of making. McNamara's attitude toward the military and his centralization of power in the Office of the Secretary of Defense caused a great furor among the military hierarchy. Because of their opposition to his methods, he virtually had to replace the entire Joint Chiefs of Staff. Although some military leaders appreciated McNamara's willingness to increase the size of the defense budget by 25 percent above the level of the Eisenhower years and his early support for and public defense of the war in Vietnam, they were in the minority and their feelings were shortlived. When McNamara turned against the war and fought against two of the military's most cherished weapon systems, the ABM and the manned bomber, and—in order to conceal the true cost of the war—postponed many routine equipment overhauls, stretched out the purchase of new systems, and cannibalized weapons stocks in Europe, the entire military hierarchy was outraged. Thus, in addition to the changed external environment, the military hierarchy was confronted internally with a decision-making process that virtually ignored military experience and a defense establishment with outmoded equipment and insufficient supplies. Both morale and materiel were in poor shape by the time of the Tet offensive.[22]

Cost Overruns

The public image of the Pentagon also began to suffer during the Vietnam War because of poor management practices which resulted in huge cost overruns and badly designed weapons systems. The two most flagrant examples during the 1960s were the giant C-5A cargo plane and the joint service fighter-bomber aircraft, the TFX (Tactical Fighter Experimental) or as it was later designated, the F-111. The Air Force originally planned to purchase 115 C-5As at an estimated cost of $2.6 billion, or a unit cost of $23 million, from the Lockheed Aircraft Corporation. Eventually, the Air Force had to settle for 77 C-5s at a total cost of $4.5 billion, or a unit cost of almost $60 million—a cost growth of 261 percent. The entire program was so poorly designed and implemented that even with the higher price of the C-5 Lockheed needed a government-backed loan to avert bankruptcy. Moreover, the planes cannot carry anywhere near their planned load, nor will the aircraft last as long as anticipated. The C-5A originally was designed to carry 220,000 thousand pounds of cargo and fly 30,000 hours. The plane is actually capable of carrying only 174,000 pounds and its flying life is 8,750 hours. The Pentagon is presently in the midst of a ten-year program of strengthening the wings of the C-5A at a cost of $1 billion. This will bring the total cost of the C-5A program to $5.5 billion or $72 million per plane, more than 300 percent above the original estimate.

The F-111 was to be a joint Air Force-Navy plane. The original plan was to buy 1,726 of these aircraft at a total cost of $4.8 billion, or $2.8 million per aircraft. However, by the time the plane reached the production stage, it was found to be totally unsuited for use by the Navy, and Congress refused to appropriate funds for the Navy version of the F-111. The Air Force eventually purchased only 519 of these aircraft for $7.6 billion, or $14.7 million per unit. Thus its cost growth was about 525 percent. Moreover, like the C-5A, the F-111 never lived up to its expectations. When these General Dynamics fighters were first placed into use in Vietnam, they began to disappear for no apparent reason and had to be grounded time after time. The joint service fighter bomber proved to be neither joint nor effective.[23] It is too small to be an effective bomber and too large to maneuver as a fighter. Today, the Air Force has only 300 of these aircraft in operational status.

In addition to cost growth in the area of weapons systems, DOD consistently underestimated the cost of the war in Vietnam. Despite the fact that the Secretary of Defense transferred huge sums of money from the baseline budget into Vietnam War accounts, the Pentagon had to ask for five consecutive supplements to its already large budgets. Between FY 1965 and FY 1969, DOD received more than $20 billion in supplements simply to prosecute the war in Southeast Asia.

Cost overruns on weapon systems such as the C-5A and F111 and the Vietnam supplements further eroded the image of the Pentagon and undermined its credibility in the dark days of the late 1960s.

Domestic Violence

All of the problems faced by the military establishment in the 1960s were not of its own making. During the war in Vietnam events were taking place within the domestic and international arenas which would have a profound effect on the position and prestige of the Pentagon. In the United States, there was a massive outbreak of violence, especially in the cities and on college campuses; internationally, this nation was moving toward accommodations with the Soviet Union and China.

The first urban riots in this country took place in the Watts section of Los Angeles in the summer of 1963.[24] Initially, many analysts believed that the Watts riots were an isolated occurrence brought about by the peculiar problems of the Los Angeles area, for example, lack of public transportation. It was also in 1963 that violence first came to America's college campuses when armed forces were called in to quell a demonstration at the University of California in Berkeley. Many people also felt that the violence at Berkeley was an isolated occurrence. However, throughout the rest of the decade, violence spread from the Pacific shores to cities and campuses across the nation.

In July 1964, less than two weeks after the enactment of the Civil Rights Act of 1964, black rioters went on a rampage in Harlem and Brooklyn. In the days that followed other race riots broke out in Rochester, New York, and in Jersey City, Elizabeth, and Patterson, New Jersey. It was while the nation's attention was riveted on these trouble spots that U.S. Navy destroyers were allegedly attacked in the Gulf of Tonkin by North Vietnamese patrol boats.

As Lyndon Johnson would later remark, "No one could then predict the scope of the problems that the riots or the Tonkin Gulf incident represented. . . ."[25] However, these incidents would prove to have dramatic implications for the military and together would contribute to the decline in the privileged position of the armed forces in our society. Tonkin Gulf would mark the watershed for American involvement in Vietnam. In response to these alleged attacks, this nation undertook a massive bombing campaign of North Vietnam. When that did not succeed in breaking Hanoi's resolve, the United States poured nearly 600,000 men into South Vietnam. As was already discussed, this intervention in Vietnam nearly destroyed the prestige, morale, and credibility of the American military.

Similarly, the violence at home spread quickly. Newark, Detroit, Chicago, Washington (D.C.), Baltimore, Pittsburgh, Kansas City, Trenton, Youngstown, and Jacksonville were among the cities that were badly damaged by outbreaks of violence. Columbia, Harvard, Yale, and Kent State were among the universities which experienced violent demonstrations. Although it is difficult to make a direct connection between the urban and campus violence and the war in Vietnam, there is little doubt that they are related.[26] Moreover, from the viewpoint of the Pentagon this domestic violence would be as harmful as Vietnam. Our domestic difficulties had an adverse impact on the Department of Defense in four ways.

First, many of these riots got so far out of hand that it became necessary to use military force to restore order. The presence of uniformed soldiers in our major cities and on college campuses transformed the image of the American military. In the minds of many, they became identified with the grievances that caused the violence. Although, except in Detroit where Lyndon Johnson sent in the Eighteenth Airborne Corps, the soldiers were members of the National Guard rather than the regular forces, this distinction was lost on the average citizen. Moreover, since most of the military men were ill equipped and trained for this type of mission, their involvement usually exacerbated the situation. The killing and wounding of several students at Kent State University by members of the Ohio National Guard outraged the nation and inflamed antimilitary feeling.

The frequent use of military force within the United States during the 1960s had another negative outcome for the Pentagon. Because the Department of Defense felt it necessary to be prepared to intervene in domestic violence in major cities, the Army was directed to gather intelligence on potential perpetrators of violence. Upon receipt of this directive, the Army zealously began to compile dossiers on all those who "in its opinion" might precipitate trouble. Because there were no controls on who might be a source of trouble, the Department of Defense amassed a great amount of information on people whose only "crime" was that they were outspoken in their opposition to the war. Included in this list were many prominent men and women in business, public, and academic life. When the existence of this military spy operation came to light, many people became further concerned about the power of the Pentagon.

A second adverse effect of the violence in America during the 1960s was the impetus it gave to moving away from the draft to an all-volunteer force (AVF). In the 1968 presidential campaign both the Democratic and Republican candidates pledged to end conscription. Humphrey and Nixon recognized that much of the violence on the campuses was a result of a system which forced young men to fight a war to which they were opposed. The candidates also realized that once this opposition abated, the President would have some breathing room to attempt to negotiate a satisfactory solution to the war in Southeast Asia. Thus, the American military was put on notice that regardless of the outcome of the 1968 presidential election, the draft would be phased out, and in the future the Pentagon would have to compete for manpower in the marketplace. As a result of campus violence, the Department of Defense would no longer be assured of a steady, inexpensive, and high-quality source of manpower.

A third effect of domestic violence was to focus the attention of Americans on unsolved problems within the United States. Many people began to question whether this nation had reversed its priorities, that is, paid too much attention and devoted too many resources to providing a military response to communism. For example, between 1964 and 1968, the federal government spent nearly $200 billion to "save Vietnam from Communism" and less than 10 percent of that amount to deal with the massive problems of our cities.

Fourth, the domestic violence accelerated the trend toward large government-funded social welfare programs. President Johnson responded just as strongly to the riots in the cities as he had to the attacks in Tonkin. Prodded by the outbreaks of violence, he declared a "War on Poverty" in America and announced plans to create "the Great Society." Legislative proposals spewed forth from the White House almost as rapidly as bombs fell from our aircraft. In 1964, Congress enacted the Food Stamp and Urban Mass Transit programs. The next year saw passage of the Medicare, Anti-Poverty, Manpower Training, Clean Air, and Water Pollution programs and a dramatic Social Security increase. In 1966, the federal government established such programs as Model Cities, Rent Supplements, and Child Nutrition. The last two years of the Johnson administration saw the enactment of another Social Security increase and the passage of the Safe Streets, Vietnam Veterans' benefits, School Breakfasts, and Fire Safety programs. Although many of these programs were unable to achieve their goals, they did create a new set of expectations among the American people regarding the social services "owed" them by the federal government.

These new expectations became critical for the Pentagon. As a result of the Great Society initiatives and the War on Poverty, the federal government had committed itself to a number of programs whose costs were open-ended or relatively uncontrollable, that is, if a person or group established eligibility for the program the government had to pay the benefits. In the euphoria of mid-1960s when our economy was expanding rapidly, very few administrators or congressmen gave sufficient thought to the ultimate costs of these programs and they easily became law. However, as indicated in Table 2, when by FY 1968 these uncontrollables crossed the $100 billion threshold for the first time and reached $107.2 billion, or 59 percent of the entire federal budget, political leaders began to take note of this new phenomenon. When projections showed that these expenditures would more than double within a decade, the attention of political leaders focused still more on the situation. The problem could be handled in one of four ways: change the laws which established the programs, raise taxes, increase the budget deficit, or reduce the controllables. The first three courses of action seemed politically and economically unrealistic in the "stag flation" that existed in the late 1960s. Thus, attention focused on the controllables. In FY 1968, defense spending represented 69 percent of the controllable outlays in the federal budget, that is, it could be reduced without changing the law. Hence, as a result of the new expectations, DOD would now be faced with coping with reductions made primarily because most of its budget was controllable.

Détente and Defense

After the breakup of their World War II alliance, the United States and the Soviets became bitter adversaries. To counter the threat

Table 2 Controllability of Budget Outlays (in billions of dollars)

| | Actual | | | | | | | | Estimate | |
---	1967	1968	1969	1970	1971	1972	1973	1974	1975	1976
Relatively uncontrollable under present law:										
Open-ended programs and fixed costs:										
Payments for individuals:										
Social security and railroad retirement	22.5	24.8	28.3	31.3	37.2	41.6	50.7	57.6	66.6	76.6
Federal employees' retirement and insurance	3.8	4.3	4.8	5.6	6.6	7.7	9.0	10.8	13.5	15.7
(Military retired pay)	(1.8)	(2.1)	(2.4)	(2.8)	(3.4)	(3.9)	(4.4)	(5.1)	(6.3)	(6.9)
(Other)	(2.0)	(2.2)	(2.4)	(2.7)	(3.2)	(3.8)	(4.6)	(5.7)	(7.2)	(8.8)
Unemployment assistance	2.8	2.9	2.9	3.7	6.6	7.5	5.7	6.5	15.2	18.6
Veterans' benefits: pensions, compensation, education,										
and insurance............................	5.0	4.9	5.7	6.6	7.6	8.3	9.3	10.0	11.9	11.9
Medicare and Medicaid	4.6	7.2	8.9	9.9	11.2	13.4	14.1	17.2	20.9	24.1
Housing payments	.3	.3	.4	.5	.7	1.1	1.6	1.8	2.1	2.6
Public assistance and related programs..........	2.8	3.4	3.9	4.7	7.4	8.9	9.1	11.5	14.2	15.6
Subtotal, payments for individuals	41.8	47.6	54.9	62.2	77.3	88.4	99.6	115.4	144.4	169.1
Net interest..............................	10.3	11.1	12.7	14.4	14.8	15.5	17.4	21.5	23.6	26.1
General revenue sharing....................	.....	.....	.....	.....	.....	.....	6.6	6.1	6.2	6.3
Farm price supports (CCC)...................	1.7	3.2	4.1	3.8	2.8	4.0	3.6	1.0	.9	.7
Other open-ended programs and fixed costs	3.0	3.0	2.8	3.8	5.2	6.4	6.3	6.8	7.9	8.6
Total, open-ended programs and fixed costs	56.8	64.8	74.5	84.2	100.1	114.3	133.4	150.8	183.0	206.8

Outlays from prior-year contracts and obligations:[1]										
National defense	21.2	24.6	25.0	24.5	21.6	19.9	18.3	20.9	22.3	23.5
Civilian programs	15.8	17.8	16.9	17.0	18.6	19.4	21.3	22.9	26.8	30.5
Total, outlays from prior-year contracts and obligations	37.0	42.3	41.9	41.5	40.2	39.2	39.6	43.8	49.1	54.0
Total, relatively uncontrollable outlays	93.7	107.2	116.4	125.7	140.4	153.5	173.0	194.5	232.1	260.7
Relatively controllable outlays:										
National defense	46.1	52.7	52.6	51.8	51.8	53.5	52.6	53.0	56.9	63.4
Civilian programs	20.1	20.8	17.6	21.5	21.9	27.7	23.8	24.2	28.5	29.1
Total, relatively controllable outlays	66.2	73.5	70.1	73.3	73.7	81.1	76.4	77.2	85.4	92.5
Undistributed employer share, employee retirement	-1.7	-1.8	-2.0	-2.4	-2.6	-2.8	-2.9	-3.3	-4.1	-3.9
Total budget outlays	158.3	178.8	184.5	196.6	211.4	231.9	246.5	268.4	313.4	349.4

Memorandum

Percent of total outlays:										
Relatively uncontrollable under present law:										
Open-ended programs and fixed costs:										
Payments for individuals	26.4%	26.6%	29.8%	31.7%	36.6%	38.1%	40.4%	43.0%	46.1%	47.3%
Other	9.4	9.6	10.6	11.2	10.8	11.1	13.7	13.2	12.3	11.9
Total open-ended programs and fixed costs	35.9	36.3	40.4	42.9	47.4	49.3	54.1	56.2	58.4	59.2

Table 2 (continued)

				Actual						Estimate	
	1967	1968	1969	1970	1971	1972	1973	1974	1975	1976
Outlays from prior-year contracts and obligations	23.4	23.7	22.7	21.1	19.0	16.9	16.1	16.3	15.8	15.5
Total relatively uncontrollable outlays	59.2	59.9	63.1	64.0	66.4	66.2	70.2	72.5	74.2	74.2
Relatively controllable outlays	41.8	41.1	38.0	37.3	34.8	35.0	31.0	28.8	27.2	26.5
Undistributed employee share, employee retirement	-1.1	-1.0	-1.1	-1.2	-1.2	-1.2	-1.2	-1.2	-1.3	-1.1
Total budget outlays................	100.0	100.0	100.0	100.0	100.0	100.0	100.0	100.0	100.0	100.0

[1]Excluding prior year contracts and obligations for activities shown as "open-ended programs and fixed costs."

Source: *The Budget of the United States Government, Fiscal Year 1976*, pp. 354-55.

allegedly posed by Soviet expansionism, this nation adopted a policy of containment. The keystone of this doctrine was a strong military force. Without such a force, containment could only be an empty slogan.

After the Chinese entrance into the Korean War on the side of the Communist North Koreans, the United States made containment a worldwide doctrine. It publicly pledged to resist Communist expansion wherever it occurred, both in Europe and in Asia. To a large extent, it was the mindless application of this doctrine by political and military leaders that brought about the massive American involvement in Vietnam.

However, somewhat paradoxically, at the same time that the United States was plunging headlong into Vietnam, it began to move toward accommodations first with the Soviet Union and then with mainland China. Détente may be said to have begun in 1963 when the United States and the Soviet Union signed the partial nuclear test ban treaty, prohibiting all above-ground or atmospheric testing of nuclear weapons, and establishing a "hot line" between the White House and the Kremlin. Over the next five years, the United States and the USSR concluded eight more major pacts including a nonproliferation treaty, an Outer Space Agreement, and a Consular Convention. By the end of the 1960s, as the two superpowers moved toward an agreement on limiting strategic arms, analysts referred to the relaxation of tensions or accommodations between the superpowers as the "spirit of détente."

Relations with China began to thaw when the United States began its withdrawal from Southeast Asia. In his second State of the World message, President Nixon referred to the Chinese nation by its proper title, the People's Republic of China, rather than Communist China.[27] In early 1971, the Chinese invited an American ping pong team to mainland China for a series of exhibitions and shortly thereafter, Henry Kissinger, the President's Assistant for National Security Affairs, undertook a secret mission to Peking. By July 1971, President Nixon was able to inform the American people that he planned to visit the People's Republic of China in the spring of 1972.

For many Americans, tired of bearing the burdens of being the world's policemen and disillusioned by the ineffectiveness of military power in Southeast Asia, détente and ping pong diplomacy came as a welcome relief. Since the American people perceived that the United States was no longer involved in a zero sum game or an ideological struggle for the soul of mankind with the Communist world, they questioned the need for a strong military force. Americans were unaccustomed to playing the subtle game of balance-of-power politics. In the past they had created an effective military force in response only to the gravest of threats—to save the world for democracy in 1917, to react to the infamous Japanese attack on Pearl Harbor in 1941, and to protect the free world from the "godless atheists" in Moscow and Peking in the late 1940s. With no crusade to fight, the American military was now seen as a drain on resources.

Paradoxically, at the same time that the United States was moving toward an accommodation with the Communist giants, the Soviet Union and China were increasing their military power by leaps and bounds. This placed the Pentagon in the "Catch 22" position of trying to convince the American public that the Soviet Union and China posed a greater military threat with détente than without it.

A Bleak Outlook

As the 1960s came to a close, things indeed looked bleak for the American military establishment. Stuart Loory's book, *Defeated: Inside the American Military Machine*, summed up the feelings of many analysts. In Loory's view, the DOD had declined to such an extent that there was great doubt whether it could ever again be an effective instrument of policy.[28] Like the Prodigal Son, the Pentagon had squandered its inheritance. Some observers even feared that the American military was so frustrated by the new environment and its problems that something akin to the French Army revolt in Algeria was possible in this country.[29]

Conclusion

This chapter has discussed the rise and fall of the military establishment in this nation. Because of their successes in World War II and the threat posed by the forces of communism, the military enjoyed a privileged position within this nation for nearly twenty-five years after World War II. During this time the DOD was able to receive about half of the total federal budget, nearly 10 percent of our GNP, and had access to unlimited manpower resources. This situation changed rapidly during the 1960s. Ill-conceived tactics in Vietnam, battlefield atrocities, problems within the United States, and a changed international environment undermined the position and credibility of the American military.

Any attempts to meet the challenges posed by these events would be difficult. Yet the Pentagon had no choice but to respond. The remainder of this book will discuss how the Pentagon adapted to its new environment. In many ways this is somewhat of a success story; by 1975, the situation had begun to change and a new consensus was emerging over the shape of national security policy and the role of military forces in that policy.

Notes

1. The privileged position accorded our military leaders concerned many thoughtful analysts even before the Vietnam era. For example, Harold Laswell warned this nation some thirty-five years ago about the dangers of a garrison state in which "the specter of crisis shapes men's minds into the strategic mold of thought and other features of social life are given meaning insofar as they can be translated in terms of ultimate fighting effectiveness." "The Garrison State," *American Journal of Sociology*, January 1941, pp. 455-68.

2. *The Economics of Defense Spending: a Look at the Realities*, U.S. Department of Defense (Comptroller), July 1972, p. 192.

3. Anderson's appointment was a convenient way to remove him from the JCS.

4. Bruce Russett, "The Revolt of the Masses: Public Opinion in Military Expenditures," in *New Civil-Military Relations*, John Lovell and Philip Kronenberg, eds. (New Brunswick, N.J.: Transaction, 1974), pp. 61-63.

5. President Kennedy's attempt to have the defense academies adopt the Coast Guard Academy model of competitive admissions was soundly rejected by Congress because of the patronage aspect.

6. Raymond Aron, *The Imperial Republic* (Cambridge, Mass.: Winthrop, 1974), p. 92; George Liska, *Imperial America* (Baltimore: Johns Hopkins, 1967), p. 10.

7. Secretary of Defense Robert McNamara made this statement to Congress annually from 1961 to 1965.

8. Harry Magdoff, *The Age of Imperialism: the Economics of United*

States Foreign Policy (New York: Monthly Review Press, 1969), pp. 39-52, 180-88; Gabriel Kolko, *The Roots of American Foreign Policy* (Boston: Beacon Press, 1969), pp. 20, 88-131.

9. David Shoup, "Our New American Militarism," *Atlantic*, April 1969, pp. 51-56. See also (Colonel) James Donovan, *Militarism U.S.A.* (New York: Scribners, 1970).

10. One of the most trenchant criticisms of Westmoreland's tactics was made by Henry Kissinger, *American Foreign Policy* (New York: W.W. Norton, 1974), chap. 3; see also Maynard Parker, "Vietnam, The War That Won't End," *Foreign Affairs*, January 1975, pp. 352-61. For a contrasting point of view, see William Westmoreland, *A Soldier Reports* (New York: Doubleday, 1976), pp. 144-61.

11. Ernest Furgurson, *Westmoreland: The Inevitable General* (Boston: Little, Brown, 1968).

12. Letter from Lavelle to Senator John Stennis (D-Miss.), September 26, 1972. Exerpts are printed in *New York Times*, October 6, 1972, p. 5.

13. The entire blame for concentrating on inappropriate measures cannot be placed on the military. As McGeorge Bundy, the Executive Assistant for National Security Affairs to Presidents Kennedy and Johnson stated, "There was a premium on imprecision." David Halbestram, *The Best and the Brightest* (New York: Random House, 1972), p. 595.

14. For a chronicle of the abuses by military leaders, see the following books by military officers: Josiah Bunting, *The Lionheads* (New York: G. Braziller, 1972); Anthony Herbert, *Soldier* (New York: Holt, Rhinehart and Winston, 1972); William Hauser, *America's Army in Crisis* (Baltimore: Johns Hopkins, 1973).

15. These problems are summarized in "Problems in the Ranks," pp. 21-38, in *The Power of the Pentagon, Congressional Quarterly, 1972*. See also M. Scott Peck, "The Role of the Military in American Society vis-à-vis Drug Abuse," in *New Civil-Military Relations*, pp. 169-92, and Richard Gabriel and Paul Savage, *Crisis in Command* (New York: Hill and Wang, 1978), pp. 29-50.

16. Portions of the Peers Report were released by the Army in November 1974. See Haynes Johnson, "Pentagon Cites Wide My Lai Cover-up," *Washington Post*, November 14, 1974, p. A1:4.

17. Townsend Hoopes, *The Limits of Intervention* (New York: David McKay, 1969), pp. 139-224; Clark Clifford, "A Vietnam Appraisal," *Foreign Affairs*, June 1969, pp. 601-22.

18. John Hersey in "The President," *New York Times Magazine*, April 20, 1975, p. 102, describes an unsuccessful attempt by Westmoreland to secure an appointment from President Ford.

19. Clayton Fritchey, "The Public and Korea," *Washington Post*, May 27, 1975, p. A17:1.

20. Russett, "Revolt of the Masses," p. 76.

21. See, for example, Maxwell Taylor, *Swords and Plowshares* (New York: Norton, 1972), p. 408.

22. There are several excellent studies of civil-military relations during the McNamara years. See, for example, William Kaufmann, *The McNamara Strategy* (New York: Harper and Row, 1964); James Roherty, *Decisions of Robert S. McNamara* (Coral Gables, Fla.: University of Miami Press, 1970); Clark Murdock, *Defense Policy Formulation* (Albany: State University of New York Press, 1974); Alain Enthoven and K. Wayne Smith, *How Much Is Enough?* (New York: Harper and Row, 1971); Ralph Sanders, *The Politics of Defense Analysis* (New York: Dunellen, 1973).

23. Robert Art, *The TFX Decision* (Boston: Little, Brown, 1968), is an excellent case study of the process by which the Pentagon decided to have General Dynamics build this joint fighter. J. Ronald Fox, *Arming America: How the U.S. Buys Weapons* (Cambridge, Mass.: Harvard University Press, 1974), criticizes the way in which the Pentagon procured weapons in the 1960s.

24. Lyndon Johnson, *The Vantage Point* (New York: Holt, Rhinehart and Winston, 1971), pp. 95, 109, 160-78, 538, discusses the domestic violence from the perspective of the White House.

25. Ibid., p. 95.

26. Samuel Lubell, *The Hidden Crisis in American Politics* (New York: Norton, 1971), pp. 182-219, discusses this relationship.

27. Richard Nixon, *U.S. Foreign Policy for the 1970's: Building for Peace*, The State of the World Message, February 25, 1971, p. 92.

28. Stuart Loory, *Defeated: Inside America's Military Machine* (New York: Random House, 1973), p. 386.

29. Zalin Grant, "Revolt in the Pentagon," *New Republic*, October 4, 1969, pp. 17-20.

CHAPTER 2

The Dark Days
from 1969 to 1974

Introduction

The period between 1969 and 1974 proved to be difficult for the Pentagon, for its civilian and military leaders had to adjust to the changed environment. This new climate had many facets and presented the military establishment with its most severe challenges since the pre-Korean War period when DOD had to accommodate pressures for demobilization with the demands placed on it by the Cold War. The executive branch, Congress, and members of the foreign policy elite all made new demands on DOD. Although each will be analyzed separately, it is important to note that these components are inextricably interrelated, that is, the constraints imposed upon DOD by the executive branch and the Congress resulted partially from and helped to create public opinion.

The New Environment within the Executive Branch

When Lyndon Johnson called a halt to the bombing of North Vietnam in early 1968 and began the long attempt to find a political solution to the war in Southeast Asia, the United States was spending $78 billion annually for national defense. This sum represented about 10 percent of our GNP and 44 percent of the entire federal budget.[1] As indicated in Table 3, six years later defense outlays had declined slightly. The FY 1974 defense budget called for spending only $74 billion or approximately 5 percent less than FY 1968. However, measured in constant FY 1974 dollars, defense spending had actually declined significantly. Thus, by FY 1974, the Pentagon had $44 billion or 37.2 percent less buying power than in 1968. Moreover, the priority given to defense also declined markedly. By FY 1974, DOD's share of the GNP had dropped to 5.8 percent while

Table 3   Defense Outlays, FY 1968 to FY 1974 (in billions of dollars)

	1968	1969	1970	1971	1972	1973	1974	% Change
Outlays (Current Dollars)	78	79	79	76	76	77	74	-5.1
Outlays (Constant FY 1974 Dollars)	118	110	103	94	86	80	74	-37.2
Percentage GNP	9.5	8.7	8.1	7.7	6.9	6.2	5.8	-38.9
Percentage Total Budget	42.5	40.6	38.4	35.5	31.7	29.0	28.2	-33.6

Source: *The Budgets of the United States Government.*

its share of the federal budget had fallen to 28.2 percent. Compared to FY 1968, this represented a 39 percent decline in the defense portion of the GNP and a 34 percent drop in the Pentagon's share of the federal budget.

The problem of adjusting to this decline in the level of defense expenditures was exaggerated by a number of other factors. The post-Vietnam period saw record-high inflation rates. Between FY 1968 and FY 1974 inflation averaged over 6 percent per year. Measured in FY 1974 dollars, the FY 1968 budget was $118 billion.

Personnel costs also increased dramatically. According to the provisions of a 1967 federal law, the pay of all federal government employees was to be made comparable to that paid to those holding similar jobs in the private sector. An amendment to that law, offered by the late Mendel Rivers (D-S.C.), then chairman of the House Armed Services Committee, stipulated that the compensation of military personnel was to be adjusted at the same rate as that of other government employees. The Comparability Law and Rivers' amendment resulted in a rapid rise in personnel costs for DOD. In FY 1968, the average pay of an active duty military man was $5,780. By FY 1974, the average compensation level had risen to $10,895, an increase of $5,115, or 88 percent in just six years. The pay of civilians employed by DOD was affected similarly. In FY 1968, the average pay of the civil servant in the Pentagon was $8,057; six years later the average compensation of the civilian working for DOD had risen by $5,204, or 65 percent, to $13,261. The steep increase in personnel costs of the Pentagon in the post-1968 period is graphically illustrated in Figure 1.

Since much of the compensation of military men is in forms other than straight salary, many people are unaware of the total costs to the government of an individual serviceman. Table 4 presents typical examples of the total annual compensation for three enlisted men and three officers as of January 1975. At that time the salary or basic pay of the lowest ranking enlisted man was only $4,129, but with normal benefits his compensation or cost to the government was increased by $3,017, or 73 percent, to over $7,000. The total compensation of a sergeant was nearly $15,000 and could have been as high as $17,000 if he possessed a critical skill and was eligible for a reenlistment bonus. A high ranking enlisted man, that is, an E-8,

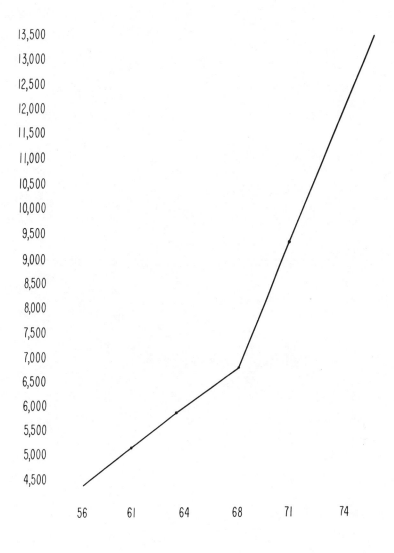

Figure 1   Average Manpower Costs for the Department of Defense, 1956-1974 (in thousands of dollars)

Table 4 Total Annual Military Compensation under Specified Conditions, Selected Examples by Grade and Rank, January 1975

	Officers			Enlisted Personnel		
	O-6 Colonel	O-4 Major	O-2 Lieutenant (junior grade)	E-8 Senior chief petty officer	E-5 Staff sergeant	E-1 Private
Years of service	26	14	2	20	4	0
Number of dependents	3	3	2	3	2	0
Duty assignment	Staff officer	Flight surgeon	Submarine	Flight deck	Munitions specialist	Basic training
Location	Germany	United States	Sea duty	Mediterranean	Thailand	United States
Compensation (dollars)						
Regular military compensation	33,743	22,132	12,984	15,171	9,348	6,156
Basic pay	27,727	17,640	9,580	11,380	6,156	4,129
Quarters allowance	3,272	2,729	2,225	2,182	1,757	760[a]
Subsistence allowance	606	606	606	880	880	880[a]
Tax advantage (average)	2,137	1,157	573	730	555	387
Special and premium pay	...	7,140	1,500	930	192	...
Medical officers						
Special pay	...	4,200	...	...	...	...
Bonus	...	(13,500)[b]	...	...	...	...
Sea and foreign duty	...	...	...	270	192	...
Selective reenlistment bonus	...	...	...	...	(2,052)[b]	...

Enlistment bonus	...	...	...	...	...	(625)[b]
Incentive pay	...	2,940[c]	...	...	...	...
Hazardous duty	...	...	1,500	660	...	...
Other pay	2,376	...	180	360	461	...
Clothing allowance	...	...	...	...	101	...
Overseas station allowance	2,376[d]	...	...[c]	...	...	...
Family separation allowance	...	...	180[c]	360	360	...
Benefits	7,312	8,591	1,594	4,786	4,766	990
Retirement	6,292	7,311	...	3,702	4,051	...
Health care	750	750	500	750	500	...
Commissary	270	530	104	334	215	...
G.I. Bill benefits	...	...	990	...	...	990
Total military compensation	43,431	37,863	16,258	21,248	14,767	7,146

Note: Because of rounding, detail may not add to totals.

a. Allowances for the recruit are based on cash rates.

b. Figures in parentheses are illustrative bonus payments and are not included in totals.

c. Flight surgeon's assignment calls for regular participation in flying duties, and submarine officer is under way half of the time.

d. Colonel is accompanied by his family and lives in private accommodations in Frankfurt, Germany. Rate shown, effective February 1975, includes a housing allowance of $4.55 a day and a cost of living allowance of $2.05 a day.

Source: Martin Binkin, *The Military Pay Muddle* (Washington, D.C.: Brookings Institution, 1975), pp. 28–29.

received more than $20,000 while the cost to the government of a junior officer was more than $16,000. A middle grade officer such as a major received $17,640 in basic pay but with certain extras his compensation could more than double to nearly $38,000. Finally, a senior officer at the O-6 or colonel level, stationed in Europe, cost the Pentagon nearly $44,000.

During this same period the Pentagon was also forced to bear the increasingly heavy burden of the military retirement system. Since military personnel are permitted to retire on half pay after only twenty years of service, the real impact of the large military force the United States had maintained since the end of World War II began to be felt only in the late 1960s. However, unlike other retirement programs run by the federal government, the military retirement system is totally unfunded, that is, non-contributory. During his years on active duty, nothing is deducted from the pay of the soldier, sailor, or marine, nor is any money placed into a trust fund by the Pentagon. Therefore, each fiscal year DOD must pay its retirees "off the top" of its budget. In FY 1964, about 400,000 people were drawing retirement pay. By 1968, the number had risen to 625,000 and by FY 1974, the number broke the 1 million barrier, an increase of 150 percent in a decade. In addition to the rise in the number of beneficiaries, the cost of the military retirement system rose substantially due to the rapid increase in the active duty base rates on which retirement is computed, and because of large consumer price index (CPI) adjustments to retirees' pay which were necessitated by inflation. In FY 1968, outlays for military retirement were about $2 billion. By FY 1974, outlays for military retirement had more than doubled to $5.2 billion, or 6 percent of the entire DOD budget. In 1972, the Pentagon attempted to alleviate the crushing burden by proposing a new retirement system, but was not able to get congressional approval for the new plan.[2]

Total personnel costs, which include military and civilian pay, military retirement, and outlays for family housing, took an ever increasing portion of the defense budget from FY 1968 to FY 1974. As is indicated in Table 5, personnel costs rose from $32.6 billion to $43 billion over this six-year period, an increase of 32 percent. The share of the defense budget devoted to personnel increased from 41.8 percent in FY 1968 to 55.2 percent in FY 1974. This dramatic

Table 5 Personnel Costs in the Defense Budget, FY 1968 to FY 1974 (in billions of dollars)

	1968	1971	1972	1973	1974
Military Personnel	19.8	22.3	23.4	23.8	24.2
Civil Service	10.3	12.2	12.5	12.8	13.8
Military Retired	2.1	3.4	3.8	4.4	5.2
Family Housing	0.4	0.5	0.6	0.6	0.8
TOTAL	32.6	38.4	40.3	41.6	43.0
Percent of Total Outlays	41.8	50.9	53.2	55.8	55.2

Source: *The Budgets of The United States Government.*

increase occurred in spite of the fact that during this period the Pentagon reduced its labor force substantially.

In addition to rapidly escalating personnel costs, DOD also had to contend with very high costs for its new weapon systems. As is indicated in Table 6, the total cost of the twenty major procurement programs underway in DOD in 1974 was more than $100 billion. Part of the high cost of these systems resulted from inflation and poor management practices. As noted in the table, the projected costs of these twenty systems had increased by 36 percent over the original estimate. However, the real driving force behind the price of new weapons systems was the high cost of technology.

The increasing costs of weapons has been a particularly critical problem in the post-1968 period because of the great need for modernization of the defense force. This acute need developed because of the actions of the Johnson administration during the height of the war in Vietnam. In a desperate effort to dampen the impact of the burgeoning costs of our involvement in Southeast Asia and to conceal the true costs of the war from the American public, the President and his advisers ordered the military to postpone or stretch out normal modernization and skip routine overhaul and maintenance projects. In addition, DOD was forced to cannibalize equipment from Europe to support the war in Southeast Asia.[3]

Table 7 presents data on the costs of present and future bombers, submarines, tactical aircraft, ships, and tanks. As shown in the table, the cost of replacing obsolete systems has risen by several hundred percent in the post-Vietnam period. Between FY 1952 and FY 1961, the United States had funded the purchase of 742 B-52 long-range manned bombers for a total cost of $5.9 billion, or a unit cost of about $8 million. The cruise missile carrier which will be a near-term replacement for the B-52 will cost approximately $100 million per plane. This represents an astonishing increase of 1,150 percent.

Between FY 1962 and FY 1971, the Pentagon funded 2,109 F-4 Phantom fighter planes for the Navy and the Air Force at a cost of $5.5 billion, or $2.6 million per aircraft. To replace the Phantom, the Navy designed the F-14 Tomcat at a cost of $24 million per unit while the Air Force developed the F-15 Eagle at a cost of $18 million per aircraft. These new aircraft will be almost six times more expensive than the F-4. The original fleet ballistic missile submarines, the

Table 6 Major Procurement Programs (in millions of dollars)

Program	Total Cost[1]	Number of Units	Unit Cost	Authorized Through FY 75	Remainder	Original Estimate	% Increase	Completion Date
Minuteman III	6,961	550	13	5769	1192	4,674	49	1979
Trident	15,446	10	1544	3033	12,413	12,431	24	1984
B-1	18,633	244	76	2027	16,606	11,218	66	1983
AWACS	2,655	34	78	1046	1609	2,661	_[2]	1980
SAM-D	6,389	N/A	N/A	853	5536	5,240	13	1990
F-14	6,307	334	19	4843	1464	6,166	2[2]	1977
F-15	10,941	749	15	4135	6806	7,355	49	1981
S-3A	3,289	187	18	2675	664	2,891	14	1977
P-3C	2,724	220	12	1840	884	1,294	111	1979
F-16	4,300	650	7	113	2887	3,000	43	1985
UTTAS	3,402	1,117	3	240	3162	2,307	48	1986
AAH	2,513	481	5	130	2388	1,800	40	1984
SSN 688	7,863	36	218	4691	3172	5,747	37	1979
MK 48	1,557	2,000	1	1072	485	1,753	_[2]	1979
DD 963	3,599	30	120	2778	821	2,531	39	1978
PF	5,274	50	105	411	4863	3,244	62	1984
DLGN 8	1,592	5	318	1135	457	820	94	1979
XM-1	4,275	3,312	1	101	4174	3,005	42	1989
A-10	2,739	743	4	370	2363	2,489	10	1980
PHM	1,108	30	37	157	951	726	53	1982
Total	110,266			37,419	72,847	81,402	36	

1. Assumed an 11% inflation in FY 75, 8% in 76, decreasing to 4.3% in FY 80, and 3.7% thereafter.
2. Program cost increases were held down by decreasing the number of units, for example, the number of F-14s has been cut in half.

Source: SAR Program Acquisition Cost Summary, June 30, 1974, OASD (C).

Table 7 Comparison of Selected New Procurement Programs with Older Counterparts (in millions of dollars)

New Weapons System	Unit Cost	Number of Units	Total Cost	Replaces	Unit Cost	Number of Units	Total Cost	Unit Increase Amount	%
CMC[a]	104	100	10,400	B-52	8	742	5,936	92.0	1150
F-14	24	500	12,000	F-4	3	2109	5,483	21	700
F-15	18	749	14,300	F-4	3	2109	5,483	15	500
Trident	1793	14	25,100	Polaris	330	41	13,530	1463	443
DD-963	120	30	3,599	DD-800	30	14	420	90	300
XM-1	1.5	7058	10,400	M-60	0.6	5000	3,000	0.9	150

a. Cruise Missile Carrier

Sources: *Annual Reports of the Department of Defense*

Polaris boats, were procured for about $330 million each. Their replacement, the Trident submarines, will cost $1.9 billion each, an increase of 443 percent for the Navy's undersea deterrent vessel. Destroyers built by the Navy before the Vietnam War were procured for about $30 million. The new DD-963, Spruance Class destroyers, cost DOD $120 million each, a rise of 300 percent. The Army intends to procure more than 7,000 of the new Main Battle tanks, the XM-1s. These will cost $1.5 million each, a 150 percent increase over the M-60, which the Army had been buying since 1959.

Finally, the declining budget levels were not matched by a concomitant reduction in the worldwide responsibilities of our military forces. The Nixon doctrine proclaimed by the President on Guam on November 3, 1969, stipulated that this nation would honor all commitments made since the end of World War II.[4] In addition, during the post-Vietnam period the armed services had to maintain substantial numbers of forward deployed forces. The Navy had to maintain two carriers on station at all times in the Pacific and the Mediterranean. The Army and Air Force still had to base several hundred thousand troops in Europe and Korea, while the Marines had to keep a large amphibious force available for use in both the Atlantic and the Pacific.

It is important to note that until 1973 the armed services had to carry out all these tasks while still conducting operations in Southeast Asia. United States activity there did not end until 1973.

Major Initiatives

In spite of record-high inflation rates, the high cost of paying its past and present employees, and the burgeoning costs of new equipment, the Pentagon was able to maintain a credible defense posture without increasing the level of defense expenditures during the 1968-1974 period. This was possible because its leaders undertook a number of bold initiatives. For purposes of analysis these may be placed into ten categories.

First, beginning in early 1969, DOD withdrew its forces from Vietnam at the rate of about 12,000 per month and simultaneously turned the prosecution of the war over to the South Vietnamese. This process, known as Vietnamization, was first conceived and enthusiastically advocated by Secretary of Defense Melvin Laird in March

1969. Its implementation enabled DOD to cut spending in Southeast Asia from almost $29 billion in FY 1969 to $6 billion in FY 1973, a decrease of $22.8 billion, or 80 percent, before the truce agreement. Table 8 outlines the declining level of expenditures and the reduction of combat forces in Vietnam from FY 1968 to FY 1973.

Table 8   War Costs and Troop Levels for the War in Vietnam (in billions of dollars)

Fiscal Year	Full Costs SEA War	Incremental Costs	Troop Levels
1968	26.5	20.0	549,500
1969	28.8	21.5	549,500
1970	23.1	17.4	434,000
1971	14.7	11.5	284,000
1972	9.1	7.1	69,000
1973	6.0	5.2	39,000

Source: *The Economics of Defense Spending; A Look at the Realities,* Department of Defense (Comptroller), July 1972, p. 149.

Second, the Pentagon drastically reduced civilian and military personnel. In FY 1968, DOD had 3.4 million military personnel and 1.3 million civil servants in its employ. By FY 1974, the number of military personnel had decreased by 1.2 million, or 35 percent, to 2.2 million. Simultaneously, the number of civilians declined by .3 million or 23 percent to approximately 1 million. Thus, the overall manpower reduction was almost 32 percent. This brought the number of military personnel to 500,000 below its pre-Vietnam level of 2.7 million, and to its lowest point since the pre-Korean War period when the United States was demobilizing. As is shown in Table 9, if DOD had not made these drastic reductions, its military and civilian personnel costs in FY 1974 would have been $17.6 billion or 46 percent above an already substantial level of $38 billion.

Reducing military manpower by 35 percent below FY 1968 levels and 18 percent below its pre-Vietnam level, without decreasing American commitments, was accommodated in three ways by the defense hierarchy: changing the force planning doctrine, developing the total force, and increasing reliance on nuclear weapons. Pre-Vietnam force planning had been predicated upon the assumption that the military would have to be able to handle two major wars and

Table 9 Pay Costs and Manpower Trends for Selected Years (outlays in millions, manpower in thousands)

Average Strength	1968	1973	1974
Military	3,436	2,324	2,218
Civil Service	1,276	1,033	1,014
Total	4,712	3,357	3,232
Military Pay	19,859	23,246	24,165
Civil Service			
Payroll	10,281	12,494	13,812
Total	30,140	36,240	37,977
Average Cost[1]			
per person	6.4	10.8	11.8
Cost of FY 1968			
Force	30,140	50,890	55,602
Actual Costs	30,140	36,240	37,977
Savings	——	14,650	17,625

1. in thousands of dollars

Source: James Schlesinger, *Annual Defense Department Report, FY 1975,* March 4, 1974, p. 21.

one minor contingency simultaneously (2½ wars). The post-Vietnam doctrine, on the other hand, assumed that the American fighting forces would never have to wage more than one major and one minor war at the same time (1½ wars).[5]

The concept of the total force involved integration of the National Guard and reserves with the active duty component in those areas where the reserves had capabilities. Previously, the reservists had been given only a marginal role in contingency planning, but in the post-1968 period, they were totally integrated into all of the Pentagon's war plans. The DOD no longer had separate active duty and reserve components but a "total force." Table 10 outlines the functions the reserves had assumed in eight selected areas of combat capability by mid-1974. In these categories the reserves provided 37 percent of United States capabilities; in the area of tactical airlift, the reserves actually accounted for a greater percentage of the forces than the active duty components. The reservists not only provided a mobilization potential but actually took on operational assignments during their training periods.

Table 10   Integration of Guard and Reserves into the Total Force

		Percentage	
Service	**Function**	**Active**	**Reserve**
Army	Combat Forces	50	50
	Maneuver Battalions	75	25
Air Force	Tactical Airlift	44	56
	Tactical Reconnaissance	60	40
	Strategic Refueling	79	21
	Strategic Airlift	57	43
Navy	Surface Combat Ships	75	25
	Patrol Aviation	67	33
Average		63	37

Source: Office of the Assistant Secretary of Defense (Manpower and Reserve Affairs).

Greater reliance on the guard and reserves required that the readiness of these forces be increased. To accomplish this, DOD established separate guard and reserve accounts within the budget of each service and greatly increased the funding level for these accounts. In FY 1968, the guard and reserves received only $2.2 billion, or 2.8 percent of the defense budget. However, by FY 1974, this account had doubled and the "weekend warriors" were receiving $4.4 billion or nearly 6 percent of the budget. In addition, the active component transferred about $1 billion in equipment each year to the guard and reserves. Since there were approximately 900,000 reservists in drill pay status in FY 1974, the total force remained above 3 million men. Moreover, because the average annual cost of each reservist was only about one-sixth as much as that of an active duty person, the total force was about $10 billion less expensive than an active duty force of comparable size.

Increasing the role of nuclear weapons in contingency planning was a partial return to the strategic concepts of the 1950s. During the Eisenhower years, the doctrine of massive retaliation served as the intellectual underpinning of our national security policy. According to this doctrine, a conventional attack on the United States or its allies could result in a massive or nuclear response by this nation. Because this policy was criticized by many strategists for its lack of flexibility and credibility during the 1960s, nuclear weapons were assigned the role of deterrents. The official policy of the United

States during the Kennedy and Johnson years was that this nation would not initiate nuclear war. To compensate for deemphasizing the role of nuclear weapons, the size of our conventional forces was increased substantially in the 1960s.[6]

However, the decrease in manpower levels in the post-1968 period reduced the size of our conventional forces well below the levels of the 1950s. This caused military leaders to wonder if this nation had sufficient forces to deter conventional attacks on such areas as Europe and Korea. To compensate for this, Secretary of Defense James Schlesinger made public statements to the effect that this nation would possibly resort to the use of nucelar weapons to repel conventional attacks.[7] To improve the credibility of this threat, Schlesinger openly sought funds for the purpose of increasing the accuracy of our nuclear forces and for improving our credibility to fight limited nuclear wars.[8] In 1975, President Ford confirmed this new emphasis on nuclear weapons by stating that the United States had renounced its policy of not being the first to use nuclear weapons.[9]

The third step that DOD took to keep its budget from increasing was to accelerate the phasing out of its older weapons systems. This action reduced operating costs and freed up funds to purchase new weapons. However, it also drastically reduced our tactical or general purpose force inventory. By FY 1974, the amount of equipment possessed by each of the services was not only far below the FY 1968 level but had dropped substantially below the 1964 or pre-Vietnam level. These changes in the weapons inventory are outlined in Table 11. The number of long-range bomber squadrons in the Air Force was reduced from 40 in FY 1968 to 28 by the end of FY 1974. This represented a decline of 30 percent and brought the 1974 level to about one-third of the 1964 level. The Air Force also substantially reduced its tactical aircraft squadrons. In FY 1968, it had 103 fighter and attack squadrons. By 1974, the number of air units had dropped by 27 percent to 75. This was 12 percent below the pre-Vietnam level of 85. However, the greatest reduction for the Air Force came in the area of fighter interceptor squadrons. In 1964, there were 40 of these units; by 1968, the number had dropped to 26 and in 1974 there were only 7 interceptor squadrons still active. This represented a drop of nearly 83 percent over the ten-year period. Overall, the number of

Table 11   Summary of Weapons Inventory, 1964-1974

Weapons System	End of Fiscal Year			Percentage Change	
	1964	1968	1974	1968-1974	1964-1974
Squadrons					
Long Range Bombers	78	40	28	-30	-64
Fighter Attack	85	103	75	-27	-12
Fighter/Interceptor	40	26	7	-73	-83
Total Squadrons	203	169	110	-35	-46
Number					
Aircraft Carriers	24	23	14	-39	-42
Amphibious Assault	133	157	65	-59	-51
Sealift	101	130	37	-72	-63
Surface Warships	368	387	187	-52	-49
Strategic Submarines	21	41	41	0	+95
Nuclear Attack	19	33	61	+85	+221
Support	266	205	90	-56	-66
Total Ships	932	976	495	-49	-47
Number					
Army Divisions	16	19	13	-32	-19
Marine Divisions	3	4	3	-25	0
Total Divisions	19	23	16	-30	-16

Sources: *Annual Defense Reports* and *Military Posture Statements.*

squadrons in the Air Force declined from 169 in FY 1968 to 110 in FY 1974, a cut of 35 percent over the six-year period. This reduction brought the total number of squadrons to about 46 percent below its FY 1964 level of 203.

The Navy also experienced severe reductions. Between FY 1968 and FY 1974, the number of attack carriers declined by 43 percent (from 23 to 13); the number of amphibious assault ships was cut by 59 percent (from 157 to 65); the number of other major surface combatants was slashed by 52 percent (from 387 to 187); and the number of support ships, that is, troopships, cargo ships, and tankers, declined by 72 percent (from 130 to 37). Overall, the number of commissioned ships in the fleet dropped from 976 to 495, a decline of 481 ships, or 49 percent, in just six years. This was the lowest level the American fleet had reached since before World War II. The only types of vessels that did not experience a reduction during this period were the strategic and attack nuclear submarines. The number of fleet ballistic missile submarines remained level at 41, while the number of nuclear attack submarines nearly doubled, increasing from 33 to 61.

The Army suffered a dramatic decline as well. In FY 1968, the nation's senior service was composed of 19 divisions, but by the end of FY 1974, the number of divisions had been reduced by 32 percent to 13. This was three divisions below that of the pre-Vietnam level of 16 divisions. Even the elite Marine Corps was not spared in this force reduction. The Marines were forced to deactivate one division and two fighter squadrons between FY 1968 and FY 1974. This left the Marines with 3 divisions and 26 fighter squadrons, somewhat below its 1964 level. The levels of weapons inventories for 1964, 1968, and 1974 are summarized in Table 11.

Fourth, to reduce partially the high cost of replacing 175 obsolete weapons systems, DOD instituted the "hi-lo mix" concept, a plan that has been widely used in the area of tactical aircraft. Instead of replacing a tactical aircraft such as the F-4 with the high performance Navy F-14 Tomcat or Air Force F-15 Eagle, the Pentagon is buying only limited quantities of these systems, that is, 500 Tomcats and 749 Eagles. The DOD is filling out the remainder of its tactical fighter inventory by purchasing the lower cost and less sophisticated F-16, F-18, and A-10 aircraft. These aircraft do not have the performance capabilities of either the F-14 or the F-15, but their cost is substantially less.

The F-16 is a lightweight, subsonic, single engine, visual combat fighter that has a unit cost of $10.8 million, or 39 percent less than that of the F-15. The Air Force plans to buy 1,388 of these planes for $15.2 billion. The F-18 is a twin engine, subsonic, visual combat fighter that has a unit cost of $17.6 million. This is $5.6 million or 24 percent less than the price of an F-14. Eventually, the Navy and Marine Corps hope to purchase 1,366 of these planes. The A-10 is a single seat, subsonic aircraft specifically designed for close air support of ground troops. Its unit cost will be only $6.3 million, 64 percent less than the F-15. The DOD is purchasing 733 of these for the Air Force. The total cost of these 3,487 "lo-cost" aircraft will be $35.7 billion. If the Pentagon were to procure 3,487 "hi-cost" F-14s and F-15s instead of these lo-cost aircraft, the price would have been almost $70 billion. Thus, the hi-lo mix has resulted in a savings of about $35 billion. To put it more realistically, for $35.7 billion the

Table 12 Hi-Lo Mix Systems in Tactical Aircraft

"Lo" Program	Number of Units	Program Cost[1]	Unit Cost[2]	Replaces	Number of Units	Program Cost[1]	Unit Cost[2]
F-16	1,388	13.8	10.8	F-15	749	13.2	17.6
F-18	1,366	17.4	17.6	F-14	500	12.1	23.8
A-10	733	4.5	6.3	F-15	749	13.2	17.6
TOTAL	3,487	35.7	10.2[3]		1,249[4]	25.3[4]	19.5[3]

1. in billions of dollars
2. in millions of dollars
3. average of all programs
4. F-15 counted only once

Source: SAR Program Acquisition Cost Summary, February 14, 1977, Office of the Secretary of Defense (Comptroller).

Pentagon could purchase only 1,830 Tomcats and Eagles rather than 3,487 F-16, F-18, and A-10 aircraft. Thus the lo-mix strategy enables DOD to add 1,679 aircraft to its inventory. Table 12 contains a comparison of the hi-lo mix for tactical aircraft.

Fifth, the Pentagon held down its unit replacement costs by pursuing a vigorous arms export policy. Because the research and development costs of a weapons system are fixed, the only way to decrease unit costs is to increase the number of units produced. Thus, DOD has sold 80 of the F-14 aircraft to Iran, 350 of the F-16 fighters to our NATO allies, 100 F-18s to West Germany, and an undetermined number of F-15s to Israel and Saudi Arabia. In FY 1975 alone, the United States sold $9 billion worth of military hardware to seventy foreign countries, an increase of 347 percent over the 1968 level of $2.7 billion.[10]

Sixth, DOD cut its overhead or support costs by reducing its base infrastructure. Between FY 1968 and FY 1974, the Pentagon closed more than five hundred of its military installations in the United States and made more than two thousand installation reductions or realignments worldwide. The Pentagon also reduced the number of troops stationed overseas from 1.2 million in 1969 to .5 million in 1974, a reduction of 58 percent. These two steps resulted in an annual savings of about $5 billion.

Seventh, the Pentagon has given many of its existing components additional roles. For example, the Marine Corps is no longer being trained exclusively for amphibious operations in the Pacific. A portion of the corps is being reoriented toward the central front of the European theater and in case of an attack on Western Europe will be used as a backup to Army divisions in the area. This has allowed the NATO commander to strengthen his northern flank, which is NATO's most vulnerable spot.[11] Similarly, DOD has expanded its capacity to maintain control of the seas by training existing Air Force units for a wide range of naval support operations. These Air Force units augment the Navy's capability to search for and identify enemy shipping, engage in jamming of radar, attack surface ships, and lay mines. This increased capability is vital because of the rapidly increasing power of the Russian surface and submarine fleets.[12] Finally, the Marines use their aircraft to augment Navy carrier wings as necessary to help offset the decline in the number of Navy planes.

Eighth, the Department of Defense improved its management practices, particularly in the area of weapons procurement. Under the leadership of successful businessman David Packard, the Deputy Secretary of Defense from 1969 to 1972, the Pentagon instituted a "fly before buy" concept of weapons procurement. To avoid disasters such as the C-5A and F111, the military services now have milestones or checkpoints at each major step in the acquisition process. These checkpoints are set up at the following stages: the beginning of a major effort in advanced development, the start of full-scale development, and the time when production of the system is authorized. Before committing itself to a complete program, DOD can cancel the program with only a minimum loss of funds if the project has not lived up to expectations.[13] No such checks existed with the C-5A and F-111.

Ninth, DOD substantially increased the number of women it recruited into the armed services. As indicated in Table 13, in 1968 there were only 25,000 enlisted women in an armed force that numbered over 3 million. By 1975, the number of female enlisted personnel had increased to 83,000 and accounted for almost 5 percent of the entire force. Moreover, by 1983, the Pentagon expects to have almost 200,000 women in its ranks. This will mean that women will compose more than 11 percent of the total population of this nation's armed services.

Raising the percentage of women in the military has been made possible by an increase in the type of jobs open to women. The DOD now permits women to serve on ships, in missile silos and maintenance battalions, and to fly aircraft. These actions not only are in keeping with the spirit of equal opportunity but actually hold down the cost of the all-volunteer force. Because the number of males eligible for military service is declining rapidly, base pay and other attractions for men probably would have had to be increased to compensate for the drop in supply. By opening up more jobs to women, the Pentagon has offset the decline in the male population without increasing its personnel costs.

Tenth, the military services have also alleviated manpower supply problems by dramatically increasing the percentage of blacks in their ranks. In 1969, blacks comprised about 9.6 percent of the enlisted personnel in our armed forces. By 1975, the percentage of black

Table 13   Female Enlisted Personnel in the Armed Services for Selected Fiscal Years (in thousands)

Service	Fiscal Year											
	1968		1970		1972		1975		1978		1983	
	No.	%	No.	%	No.	%	No.	%	No.	%	No.	%
Army	11	0.8	12	1.0	12	1.8	38	5.6	51	7.5	80	11.8
Navy	6	0.8	6	1.1	6	1.2	18	3.8	20	4.4	40	8.7
Marine Corps	3	0.9	2	0.9	2	1.2	3	1.6	4	2.1	7	4.2
Air Force	6	0.8	9	1.4	12	1.9	25	5.0	42	8.9	72	15.6
DOD	25	0.8	28	1.1	32	1.6	83	4.6	117	6.5	199	11.1

Source: Assistant Secretary of Defense (Manpower, Reserve Affairs and Logistics), *Manpower Requirements Report for FY 1979*, February 1978, p. vx-1.

enlisted personnel had risen to 16.3 percent, and in 1977 blacks comprised about 18 percent of the total number of enlisted personnel. Between 1969 and 1977, while the size of the military services dropped by 1.4 million, or 41 percent, the number of black enlisted personnel actually increased by 43,000, that is, from 277,000 to 320,000, or 16 percent. Figure 2 illustrates the increase of blacks in the armed services in the 1969-1977 period.

While high unemployment among black youths no doubt contributed to attracting blacks to the military, other factors were operating. Chief among these were the attitudes and actions of the Pentagon leadership. Recognizing that it was making poor use of a large reservoir of extremely valuable manpower, the military made extensive efforts to recruit in areas heavily populated by blacks. In addition, the armed services concentrated on eliminating racism and opening up opportunities for advancement to minorities. While DOD still has a long way to go toward accomplishing these goals, it has made some progress. For example, the number of black officers in the four armed services more than doubled between 1969 and 1977, increasing from 1.6 percent to 3.7 percent. The number of black noncommissioned officers (NCOs) also doubled in that same period, and the reenlistment rate among blacks was twice as high as that among whites.

Between 1968 and 1974, DOD also took a number of less spectacular but significant steps. It decreased the number of senior officers by 10 percent, increased the enlisted to officer ratio and the ratio of combat to support troops, increased tour lengths, reduced the number of transients, cut off flight pay to senior officers in non-flying billets, consolidated training activities, cut the size of headquarters staffs, eliminated or consolidated twenty major commands, slashed the number of officers receiving fully funded graduate education by 30 percent, and reduced the number of pilots trained per active aircraft by 25 percent. None of these programs in itself saved vast sums of money, but when added together the resulting cumulative savings were quite substantial.

The full extent of these savings can be seen by examining the support or overhead costs in the defense budget. Support costs are contained primarily in three program categories: training, medical, and general personnel; central supply and maintenance; and admin-

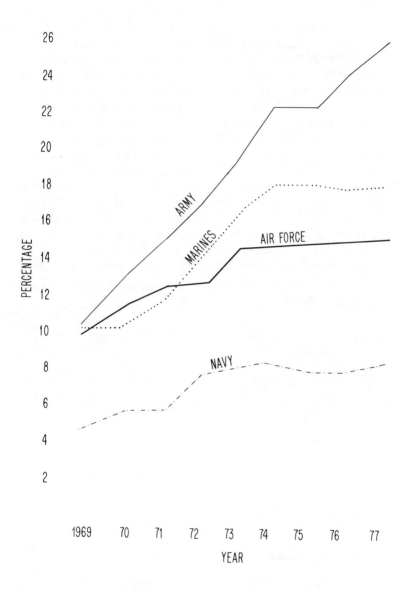

Figure 2   Percentage of Blacks in the Armed Services, 1969-1977.
Source: Department of Defense.

istration. As indicated in Table 14, these costs rose by $4.9 billion, or 25 percent, in the FY 1968-1974 period. However, in constant FY 1974 dollars these costs have declined by $4 billion, or by 14 percent. This real decrease resulted from implementation of some of the programs discussed. Without these actions support costs would have shown a sharp increase even in real terms because of inflation and the rising costs of personnel and materials. Through them DOD was able to maintain a credible defense posture within a budget that was level in current dollars and decreasing in constant or real terms. However, the fiscal constraints imposed by the executive branch were not the only challenges faced by the Pentagon during the post-1968 period. The DOD also had to contend with a number of influential individuals and groups from both the Congress and the public, who urged the creation of a significantly smaller defense establishment.

Table 14   Support Costs in the Defense Budget for Selected Fiscal Years (in billions of dollars)

Category	1968	1970	1972	1973	1974	Change $	Change %
Training, Medical and General Personnel[1]	10.1	10.9	11.4	12.0	13.6	+3.5	35
Central Supply and Maintenance	8.4	9.1	8.3	8.7	8.9	+0.5	6
Administration	1.2	1.5	1.6	1.7	2.1	+0.9	75
Total (current dollars)	19.7	21.5	21.3	22.4	24.6	+4.9	25
Total (constant FY 1974 dollars)	28.6	27.8	25.2	24.9	24.6	-4.0	-14

1. Excludes military retirement

Source: David Ott, Lawrence Korb et al., *Public Claims on U.S. Output* (Washington, D.C.: American Enterprise Institute, 1973), p. 42.

The Congressional Challenge

During the late 1960s, public opinion regarding the need for high levels of defense spending underwent a dramatic shift. This was brought about primarily by widespread disillusionment with United States involvement in Vietnam and by a new awareness of the major problems existing at home. These shifts in public attitude had a profound impact on Congress and undermined the once-favored relationship between Capitol Hill and DOD.

From the outbreak of the Korean War through the Tet offensive of 1968, DOD enjoyed a special relationship with the Congress. One indication of this was the way in which the Hill handled the defense budget. Compared to the non-defense agencies of the federal government, the Pentagon's budget requests were almost always treated quite kindly by the legislative branch. As indicated in Table 15, in the

Table 15 Congressional Changes in Budget Requests, FY 1950 to FY 1969 (in percentages)

Administration	Fiscal Year	Total Budget	Defense Budget	Non-defense
Truman	1950	-4.0	-2.3	-4.8
	1951	-2.4	-0.1	-3.6
	1952	-4.6	-1.0	-12.0
	1953	-9.5	-11.3	-6.0
	Average	-5.1	-3.7	-6.6
Eisenhower	1954	-16.2	-3.9	-41.5
	1955	-4.6	-3.6	-6.0
	1956	-3.4	-1.1	-8.1
	1957	-0.4	+1.5	-4.2
	1958	-6.9	-1.8	-17.2
	1959	-0.8	+2.0	-6.3
	1960	-2.2	-0.1	-4.7
	1961	-0.3	+1.7	-4.1
	Average	-4.4	-0.7	-11.5
Kennedy	1962	-4.9	+0.6	-10.4
	1963	-4.2	+0.5	-8.8
	1964	-5.9	-3.7	-8.0
Johnson	1965	-3.8	-1.5	-6.0
	1966	-2.0	-0.2	-3.8
	1967	-6.4	+0.7	-13.6
	1968	-3.7	-2.3	-5.0
	1969	-8.4	-6.8	-10.0
	Average	-4.9	-1.6	-8.2
All Administrations	Average	-4.7	-1.7	-9.2

Sources: House Appropriations Committee, *Department of Defense Appropriations for 1964*, Part 2, p. 585; and OASD (C).

FY 1950-1969 period Congress reduced the overall budget requests of the executive branch by just under 5 percent. However, defense cutbacks in this period averaged only 1.7 percent while those in the non-defense section were more than five times greater (9.2 percent). Moreover, in six of those twenty years Congress actually provided increased appropriations for the Pentagon. Never did the legislators do this for the non-defense sector. On only one occasion did Congress treat the non-defense sector less harshly than the defense area. Finally, this privileged treatment for DOD applied to almost the same degree throughout each of the four post-World War II administrations.

However, beginning with the first budget presented to Congress after the Tet offensive, that is, FY 1970, the legislative branch completely reversed its attitude toward defense and non-defense programs.[14] Overall from FY 1970 to FY 1975, the Democratic-controlled legislature appropriated more money than the Republican presidents sought in four of the six years. The total impact of Congress in this period was to increase federal spending by .5 percent. However, it achieved this by slashing a full 6 percent from defense requests and adding nearly 5 percent to the non-defense portion of the budget. In contrast to its previous behavior, Congress appropriated more funds for the non-defense sector in each of the six years and reduced the defense portion each year. Congressional impact on the defense and non-defense sectors of the federal budget in the FY 1970-1975 period is presented in Table 16.

Table 16   Congressional Changes in Budget Requests, FY 1970 to FY 1975 (in percentages)

Fiscal Year	Total Budget	Defense Budget	Non-defense
1970	-1.7	-7.7	+5.8
1971	+0.7	-3.4	+2.5
1972	-4.2	-4.4	+0.1
1973	+4.7	-7.2	+10.2
1974	+0.1	-6.3	+2.4
1975	+3.3	-7.0	+7.4
Average	+0.5	-6.0	+4.7

Sources: Joint Committee on Reduction of Federal Expenditures, *1974 and 1975 Budget Scorekeeping Reports.*

The real extent of the negative congressional impact on the Pentagon during the FY 1970-1975 period is obscured if one looks only at the aggregate numbers. This occurs because much of the defense budget cannot realistically be reduced or controlled by Congress. During these years about 55 percent of the defense total was allocated to pay and allowances of personnel. These items are fixed by law and must be paid. Another 15 percent of the defense portion was consumed by routine operations and maintenance (O and M) costs. It is very difficult for Congress to deny the Pentagon the funds to purchase the necessary gas and oil for their ships, planes, and tanks or to refuse to authorize the money needed to keep the equipment in good repair. Another 10 percent of the defense budget is spent on routine or minor procurement items such as bullets and bandages. It is not feasible for the legislature to make large cutbacks in the requests for these essential items. Thus, only 20 percent of the Pentagon budget is allocated for investment, that is, major procurement and research and development, test and evaluation (R,D,T, and E). This is the only area realistically subject to more than marginal changes by the Congress.

As indicated in Table 17, in the post-1969 period Congress made only small changes in the personnel and O and M categories but attacked the investment areas with gusto. Procurement was reduced by nearly 13 percent and R and D by almost 8 percent, an average reduction of 12 percent in investment in the FY 1970-1975 period. The impact in procurement and R and D was thus more than six times greater than in the other categories.

In order to appreciate the real extent of the congressional "about face" in the post-1968 period it is necessary to distinguish between two processes. The Pentagon budget is subject to both authorization and appropriation by Congress. The armed services committees must authorize or approve all major investment programs before the legislature can appropriate or grant money for the programs. Traditionally, members of these committees have been among the leading advocates of a very strong national defense. Armed services committee chairmen such as Congressmen Carl Vinson (D-Ga.) and Mendel Rivers (D-S.C.) and Senators Richard Russell (D-Ga.) and John Stennis (D-Miss.) have been outspoken in their support of the Pentagon over the years. These men have felt so strongly about national

Table 17 Congressional Changes in the Defense Budget by Appropriation Category, FY 1970 to FY 1975 (in percentages)

Appropriation Category	1970	1971	1972	1973	1974	1975	Average 1970-1975
Personnel	-3.3	-1.2	-1.1	-1.9	-1.5	-2.3	-1.9
O and M	-4.3	-0.8	-1.7	-2.4	-2.7	-6.4	-3.1
Procurement	-14.6	-7.7	-9.7	-16.0	-15.4	-13.3	-12.8
R, D, T, and E	-10.4	-6.0	-5.8	-9.5	-6.2	-7.9	-7.6
TOTAL	-7.5	-3.1	-4.0	-6.6	-4.5	-7.2	-6.0

Source: OASD (C).

security that on several occasions they have not hesitated to challenge the President himself when he overruled the military in certain areas.

The most famous of these incidents occurred in March 1962 when the House Armed Services Committee, at Vinson's urging, directed the Secretary of the Air Force to spend not less than $491 million during FY 1963 on the B-70 aircraft.[15] Both the President and the Secretary of Defense had decided that the B-70 was both impractical and unneeded, but Air Force Chief of Staff Curtis LeMay persuaded Vinson that the plane, which would be a follow-on to the B-52, was vital to our strategic deterrent. As a result of pressure from Vinson and his colleagues, President Kennedy allowed three prototypes of the B-70 to be built and Secretary of Defense McNamara reexamined the program on the basis of the information gained from testing the prototype aircraft.[16]

The support of the armed services committees for DOD in the pre-Vietnam period was also demonstrated by their handling of the annual defense budget. In the FY 1962-1968 period the Pentagon requested $19 billion in authorization authority.[17] The committees not only gave them the entire amount requested but actually added $1.6 billion or 1.3 percent over the seven-year period. In only two of these seven years did they make even minor reductions in DOD's requests.

However, even these staunch Pentagon supporters changed their attitude after the Tet offensive. In the FY 1969-1975 period, the Pentagon requested $155.8 billion but received authorization for only $146.2, a reduction of $9.6 billion, or 6.2 percent. The committee thus acted six times more negatively in the post-1968 period than in the previous seven years. Moreover, in contrast to the previous period the committee made reductions in DOD's budget requests every single year. A comparison of the congressional impact in the authorization process in the pre- and post-1969 period is shown in Table 18.

To make these changes in the defense budget, Congress needed to increase the amount of information it received from DOD. The legislators accomplished this through the use of both formal and informal mechanisms. Formally, they conducted longer and more detailed hearings on defense matters, particularly the budget re-

Table 18   Congressional Impact in the Authorization Process, FY 1962 to FY 1975 (in billions of dollars)

	1962	1963	1964	1965	1966	1967	1968	TOTAL[1]	Average Change FY 1962-1968
Amount Requested	12.9	12.4	15.4	17.1	19.3	20.8	21.1	119.0	
Amount Authorized	13.5	12.9	15.3	16.9	19.4	21.4	21.2	120.6	
Amount of Change	+ 0.6	+ 0.5	- 0.1	- 0.2	+ 0.1	+ 0.6	+ 0.1	+ 1.6	+0.23
Percentage of Change	+ 4.7	+ 4.0	- 0.6	- 1.2	+ 0.5	+ 4.8	+ 0.5	+ 1.3	+1.81

	1969	1970	1971	1972	1973	1974	1975	TOTAL[1]	Average Change FY 1969-1975
Amount Requested	22.4	21.9	20.3	22.0	23.3	22.8	23.1	155.8	
Amount Authorized	21.6	20.6	19.9	19.3	20.9	- 2.8	21.0	146.2	
Amount of Change	- 0.8	- 1.3	- 0.4	- 0.7	- 2.4	- 2.0	- 2.0	- 9.6	-1.37
Percentage Change	- 3.6	- 5.9	- 2.0	- 3.2	-10.3	-12.3	- 8.7	- 6.2	-6.57

1. Totals may not add because of rounding.

Sources: *The Budgets of the United States Government.*

Table 19 Appearance of DOD Witnesses before Congress for Selected Calendar Years

	1964	1972	1974	Change 1964-1974	
				N	%
Sessions	260	370	402	142	55
Total Witnesses	630	1060	1483	853	135
Hours of Actual Testimony	650	2376	2582	1932	297
Man Hours before Congress	1575	5522	7746	6171	392
Number of Committees	24	56	68	44	183
Length of Hearings in Words	3,003,000	10,947,000	12,300,000	9,297,000	309

Source: Office of the Assistant Secretary of Defense (Legislative Affairs).

quests. As is indicated in Table 19, in 1964, the last pre-Vietnam year, Congress spent comparatively little time on DOD matters. All told, it scheduled only 260 sessions at which some 630 DOD witnesses gave about 650 hours of actual testimony. When published, these hearings amounted to about 3 million words. By 1972, Congress had increased the sessions devoted to defense matters to 370, the number of witnesses to more than 1,000, and the hours of testimony to 2,376; the length of the printed hearings ran to almost 11 million words. By 1974, the Congress was taking more than 2,500 hours of testimony from 1,483 defense witnesses at 402 sessions; the printed hearings ran to over 12 million words or approximately 120 full-length books. Compared to 1964, Congress had increased the hours of testimony and the length of hearings approximately fourfold and the number of witnesses almost threefold.

Congress also dramatically increased the informal demands that it made on the Pentagon, that is, letters and telephone calls requesting information on defense matters. As is shown in Table 20, in 1964 the total number of these inquiries was 666,000. By 1974, the number of these informal communications had climbed by more than 50 percent to just over a million.

Table 20   Congressional Inquiries for Selected Calendar Years

Congressional Inquiries[1]	1964	1973	1974	Increase 1964-1974	
				N	%
Written	98	140	152	54	55
Telephoned	568	774	855	287	51
Total	666	914	1,007	341	51

1. in thousands.

Source: Office of the Assistant Secretary of Defense (Legislative Affairs).

Congress used this massive amount of information not only to make changes in the defense budget but also to restrict the discretion that DOD has to manage internal operations. The legislature did this through the use of the "item" method of amending the defense budget. Basically, there are three types of items associated with congressional review of the DOD budget—the line item, the special interest item, and the action item. The number of these appended to the DOD budget in recent years is summarized in Table 21.

Line items are the number of subdivisions or lines in the total budget into which funds are appropriated by Congress. The executive agency has only limited authority to shift or reprogram funds between lines in the budget. Obviously, the fewer the lines, the more discretion accorded the executive. A decade ago the defense budget had only 155 line items. By FY 1975, the number had jumped to more than 720. A good example of congressional demand for increased subdivisions and more control is the Army's procurement of equipment and missiles account (PEMA). In FY 1964, funds were appropriated in one lump sum for the entire PEMA account. The Army thus could switch funds at will among its missiles, aircraft, and tracked vehicle programs. However, by FY 1975, PEMA had been replaced by five subdivisions: aircraft, missiles, weapons, tracked combat vehicles, ammunition, and other or miscellaneous. This diffusion of line items took away DOD's flexibility to switch funds among the Army's major programs as it had done in the past.

Special interest items are those areas of the budget where Congress prohibits any reprogramming at all. A decade ago Congress did not mark any items as special interest. In FY 1975, 436 items were placed into this category by the legislature. This technique forces the Pentagon to expend funds in areas where it may not wish. For example, since 1970, members of the congressional delegation from Texas have succeeded in convincing their colleagues to appropriate funds for F-111B and A-7 aircraft which are built in Dallas. Neither the Air Force nor the Navy wishes to buy any more of these planes. However, by designating these programs as special interest areas, Congress can virtually compel DOD to buy these systems. Likewise, marking an item as special interest makes it impossible for the Pentagon to hide a cost overrun in a particular program by shifting funds from another account into the problem area.

Action items are provisions that Congress adds to the authorization and appropriation bills which direct the Pentagon to take action in certain areas; these may or may not be related to the budget. A decade ago, there were 107 of these items. By FY 1975, the number of active items had increased to about 350. A few examples will show how these items can have far-reaching implications on our force posture. In one action item Congress directed the Pentagon to make all future major surface combatant ships nuclear powered. This

Table 21 Items in the Defense Budget Reports for Selected Fiscal Years

	1964	1968	1972	1975	Increase 1964-1975 N	Increase 1964-1975 %
Line Items	155	177	385	720	565	365
Special Interest	-	-	-	436	-	-
Action Items and General Provisions	107	105	130	341	234	219

Sources: *Congressional Reports Acompanying the Budget Bills.*

provision has driven the cost of the cruisers to more than $1 billion and of carriers to more than $2 billion, severely limiting the number of ships which the Navy will be able to purchase over the rest of the decade. Another action item mandated that the Navy develop a lightweight fighter that was a derivative of the F-16 fighter being built by Ling, Tempco, Vaught for the Air Force. When the Navy claimed that this was not feasible and ordered the F-18 from McDonnell-Douglas, the Ling, Tempco, Vaught Corporation filed a complaint with the General Accounting Office charging the Navy with violating this mandate of Congress.[18] (Although the Navy successfully defended itself, it had the burden of proof on itself and the F-18 program was delayed by one year.)

A third action item added by Congress ordered the nation's military academies to admit women. The services had long argued that such a step was contrary to the purpose of the military academies, that is, to train officers for combat. Since Congress did not simultaneously change the law that prohibits women from combat assignments, this action item is making it difficult for the academies to carry out their assigned mission.[19]

The Pentagon Adjusts

To adjust to this new congressional mood which sought to make large reductions in investment authority and to control Pentagon operations, DOD relied on two techniques in the FY 1968-1974 period. First, to preserve its major programs, it made use of the distinction between budget authority and outlays. Second, to live within item restrictions it has severely reduced its reprogramming but has gained some flexibility by increasing its use of the supplemental request.

As has been discussed, the defense budget is presented both in terms of authority and outlays. Budget authority is an amount of money that can be spent or obligated over a given period of time.[20] Outlays are the funds that will actually be spent in a particular fiscal year. The total of the outlays in an agency's budget is the sum of the authority remaining from previous years and that part of the new authority which will be spent in that particular fiscal year. For example, in FY 1976, DOD projected outlays of $88.5 billion. About

$20.4 billion comes from authority left over from previous years, while the other $68.1 billion is a result of new authority. For FY 1976, total budget authority amounted to $97.5 billion. The relationship between authority and outlays is depicted in Table 22.

Each fiscal year, Congress deals only with requests for authority. Its impact on outlays is indirect, that is, if it changes authority which would have been spent in the fiscal year. To minimize the impact of Congress on the investment area of defense budget, the Pentagon has had to direct congressional cuts toward those areas where the authority would not be used in the fiscal year under review. Since the funds would not be spent in that budget year, new authority could be sought in the upcoming year if reductions were in fact made.

This tactic worked quite successfully. Between FY 1970 and FY 1975, Congress cut procurement authority by $15.4 billion or nearly 13 percent. In the R and D area, Congress reduced authority by nearly $4 billion, or 7.4 percent. However, the legislature's effect on procurement and R and D outlays was significantly less. Actual outlays for procurement were reduced by only 5.4 percent, or about $6 billion, while R and D expenditures were cut back by only $1.6 billion, or 2.6 percent. The authority reduction in total investment was about $20 billion while the real impact on outlays was only $7 billion, about 70 percent less. The difference between authority and outlays in the investment area in the FY 1970-1975 period is depicted in Table 23.

The Pentagon's success in warding off major reductions is further exemplified by looking at the programs where authority was reduced. In the FY 1970-1975 period, Congress reduced authority at one time or another for the F-14 and the F-15 fighter aircraft, the DD-963 destroyer, and the Trident submarine programs. Yet because the cuts were in "future" authority, the Pentagon was able to recoup its losses by increasing the authority for these programs in subsequent years. All of these major programs were eventually fully funded. Melvin Laird, who served as Secretary of Defense from 1969 to 1973, illustrated the impact of the authority/outlays distinction by remarking that he never really lost a vote during his tenure.[21]

Table 24 outlines the reprogramming actions taken by DOD in the FY 1968-1974 time frame. Analysis of the data contained in this table shows the steep decline in the number and dollar value of reprogram-

Table 22 Department of Defense Outlay Projections (in billions of dollars)

Program Year	Program Value	1976	197T[1]	1977	1978	1979	1980	1981	1982	Later
1975 and Prior Balance	39.8	20.4	2.8	8.0	3.7	2.0	1.4	.7	.3	.5
1976	97.5	68.2	6.5	12.4	5.9	2.1	1.2	.5	.3	.4
Transition	22.5	-	12.8	5.7	2.2	1.0	.4	.2	.1	.1
1977	110.2	-	-	72.2	19.0	9.8	3.9	2.2	.8	2.3
1978	123.1	-	-	-	79.3	22.6	11.2	4.6	2.7	2.7
1979	135.4	-	-	-	-	83.8	26.3	13.9	5.9	5.5
1980	145.8	-	-	-	-	-	89.4	28.4	14.8	13.2
1981	156.7	-	-	-	-	-	-	95.1	30.7	30.9
1982	166.8	-	-	-	-	-	-	-	100.8	66.0
Grand Total		88.5	22.1	98.3	110.1	121.3	133.8	145.6	156.4	121.6

Note: Detail may not add to totals due to rounding.

1. 197T refers to the transitional period from July through September 1976, when the start of the fiscal year was changed from July 1 to October 1.

Source: Office of the Assistant Secretary of Defense (Comptroller), *National Defense Budget Estimates for FY 1978*, p. 24.

Table 23   Congressional Impact upon Defense Authority and Outlays in Procurement and R, D, T, and E, FY 1970 to FY 1975 (in millions of dollars)

| | Procurement | | | |
| | Authority | | Outlays | |
Fiscal Year	%	$	%	$
1970	-14.6	-3,045	-7.9	-1,851
1971	-7.7	-1,328	-0	+0
1972	-9.7	-1,903	-4.5	-805
1973	-15.9	-3,368	-3.0	-482
1974	-15.4	-3,111	-7.6	-1,249
1975	-13.3	-2,636	-9.6	-1,574
	-12.8	-15,391	-5.4	-5,961

| | R, D, T, and E | | | |
| | Authority | | Outlays | |
Fiscal Year	%	$	%	$
1970	-10.4	-853	-8.2	-639
1971	-5.0	-367	-1.1	-79
1972	-5.4	-430	0	0
1973	-9.2	-808	-3.8	-301
1974	-6.2	-542	0	0
1975	-7.9	-746	-2.7	-240
	-7.4	-3,746	-2.6	-1,659

Sources: *The Budgets of the United States Government.*

ming actions over that eight-year period. In FY 1968, the Pentagon initiated 171 reprogramming actions that affected 378 line items. These actions had a dollar value of $7 billion, or nearly 10 percent of the defense budget. Each year the number of actions and the dollar amount of reprogramming dropped significantly. By FY 1974, DOD was initiating only 24 reprogramming actions affecting just 37 line items. The dollar value of these actions had declined to $211 million, or .3 percent of the total budget. Thus, in seven years the number of actions had declined by 147, or 80 percent, and the dollar value had declined by $6.8 billion, or 97 percent.

On the surface it appeared that Congress had locked the Pentagon into a budgetary straitjacket once the appropriation bill had been passed. However, to obtain funds for areas in which reprogramming was impossible or impractical, DOD resorted to asking for supplemental requests. Between FY 1950 and 1964, when there were very

Table 24 Department of Defense Reprogramming Actions, FY 1968 to FY 1974 (in millions of dollars)

Requested	FY 1968	FY 1969	FY 1970	FY 1971	FY1972	FY 1973	FY 1974
Number of Actions	171	121	129	132	82	56	24
Number of Line Items	378	432	299	275	185	129	37
Dollar Value of Program	7,040	4,445	2,431	3,266	1,866	1,453	226
(Sec. 836/736/735 Transfers)	-	-	-	(348)	(803)	(789)	(85)
Approved							
Dollar Value of Program	[2]	[2]	[2]	3,146	1,680	1,255	211
(Sec. 836/736/735 Transfers)	-	-	-	(280)	(694)	(672)	(75)
Comparison							
Value of Total Defense Program[1]	72,754	76,096	74,000	71,247	74,632	76,701	79,141
% of Reprogramming Increases	9.7%	5.8%	3.3%	4.4%	2.3%	1.6%	.3%
(Excl. 836/736/735 Transfers)	-	-	-	4.0%	1.3%	.8%	.2%

1. Regular Military Function appropriations only. Excludes Military Construction, Family Housing, Military Assistance, Civil Functions, and Civil Defense.
2. Not available

Source: OASD (C).

few restrictions on reprogramming, DOD sought only $39 billion in
supplemental funds, about $2.6 billion, or 5 percent of the size of the
budget annually.[22] However, between FY 1970 and 1974, when
reprogramming restrictions became severe, the Pentagon sought $72
billion in supplemental funds, about $14 billion, or 16 percent
annually.

In order for Congress to digest the massive amounts of information from the Pentagon and make the large number of changes in the
defense budget which it deemed necessary, the legislative branch
began to spend longer and longer periods examining the defense
budget. Consequently, in the post-Vietnam period Congress was not
able to enact the defense budget before the start of the fiscal year. For
example, between FY 1970 and FY 1975, Congress could not complete action on the defense budget before the second quarter of the
fiscal year; in FY 1971, it actually delayed passage of the defense
appropriation bill until eleven days into the fourth quarter. On
average, Congress completed its review of the defense budget about
half way into each fiscal year. The actual dates on which the defense
budget has been enacted by Congress in the FY 1970-1975 period are
in Table 25.

The repeated failure of Congress to report out a final budget
before the start of the fiscal year had forced the Pentagon to operate
under a continuing resolution, that is, to spend at the same rate as the
previous year. This has led to a great many inefficiencies in Department of Defense management. In those areas where the final budget
differed from the previous year, the Pentagon had only one half of
the year or less to adjust the account. Moreover, since the Department of Defense must complete action on its upcoming budget
request during the fall, the Pentagon leadership was placed in the
difficult position of having to decide on next year's budget without
knowing the previous year's. These uncertainties added about 3 to 5
percent to the annual costs of operating the military structure.[23]
Most members of the Comptroller's Office in the Pentagon would
have preferred an on-time appropriation, even if it were up to 5
percent below the actual level of the late appropriations.

In 1974, because of complaints from members of the Pentagon
hierarchy and other sectors of the government and the informed
public about the manner in which it dealt with the budget, Congress

Table 25 Dates on Which DOD Budget Was Passed by Congress

	Fiscal Year						Average
	1970	1971	1972	1973	1974	1975	1970-1975
Date of Basic Appropriation	29 Dec.	11 Jan.	18 Dec.	26 Oct.	20 Dec.	8 Oct.	16 Dec.
Days of Fiscal Year Elapsed	183	194	172	157	174	139	170
Percentage of Fiscal Year Elapsed	50	53	47	43	48	38	47

Source OSD (C) PAD.

passed the Congressional Budget Impoundment and Control Act. This comprehensive act, which Speaker of the House Carl Albert (D.-Okla.) called the most significant congressional initiative in seventy-five years, has three main features.[24] First, effective in 1976 it postponed the start of the fiscal year from July to October, thus giving the legislature nine months to complete action on appropriation bills. Second, it set rigid timetables for enactment of the appropriation bills and prohibited Congress from adjourning until it completed action on all fiscal matters. Finally, the act established a budget committee in each house with responsibility for setting spending and revenue totals, that is, establishing economic policy. To assist these new committees, the act set up a Congressional Budget Office (CBO), a nonpartisan group of budget analysts charged with providing the legislature with that same type of expertise on budgetary issues which the Office of Management and Budget offers to the White House.

The Congressional Budget Act has proved to be a mixed blessing for the Pentagon. It has eliminated one problem but created another. Because the start of the fiscal year has been delayed for three months and rigid timetables have been established, the Department of Defense now has its budget completed before the start of the fiscal year. It thus can save several billion dollars annually through the elimination of uncertainty.

However, the newly created budget committees in each house have created new difficulties for DOD. Under the system, the committees set a target for the overall federal budget and for each program within the budget before the traditional old-line groups such as Armed Services deal with the budgetary requests of the individual agencies. Since the budget committees are dominated by people less sympathetic to defense than those legislators on the armed services and defense appropriation committees, the defense budget is treated more harshly than it would otherwise be.[25] This new situation was demonstrated vividly during the 1975 congressional session. The budget committees set a target that reduced defense spending by 6.5 percent while raising the non-defense portion by 21.1 percent. The Senate and House Armed Services Committees ignored the defense ceiling and agreed on a defense authorization bill that exceeded (by about $1 billion) the target set by the budget committees. When the conference bill reached the Senate floor, it was defeated by a 48-42 margin, the first time that the Senate has overturned a conference defense bill. The armed services committees were forced to go back into conference and report out a new bill that conformed more closely to the budget target. This lesson was not lost on the defense appropriations subcommittees in either house. Both the Senate and the House committees stayed within the ceilings during the appropriations process and rejected all requests from Pentagon leaders to restore portions of the cuts. As a result, the defense budget for FY 1976 eventually received a cut of $7.5 billion, or nearly 8 percent, the largest absolute or percentage reduction in history. The pattern continued the following year. The budget committees raised the non-defense portion $21 billion and reduced defense by $2.8 billion.

The new budget committee in effect subjects the defense budget to triple jeopardy. Before the Pentagon can spend any money, funds must be authorized, then appropriated, and now subjected to target limitations. The more scrutiny to which the defense budget is subjected, the more likely it is to be reduced, for the defense budget is the most complex, visible, and controllable budget in the entire federal government.

The McGovern Challenge

Despite the real decline in the level of defense expenditures in the post-1968 period, the decreasing priority being given to defense, and the increased control over Pentagon affairs exercised by the Congress, there were a number of prestigious groups and individuals in American society who claimed that the Pentagon was not reducing its forces quickly enough to conform to the realities of the post-Vietnam era. After the defense budget was presented to the Congress each year, there were a number of alternative defense budgets prepared. Some of the groups proposing these alternative defense budgets, with recommendations for spending cuts, included the National Urban Coalition, the Project on Budget Priorities, the Center for Defense Information, and the Brookings Institution. These alternative budgets with their suggested savings received a sympathetic hearing in the Congress, the national media, and the academic community because of the individuals associated with these groups. The Project on Budget Priorities was headed by Paul Warnke, Assistant Secretary of Defense for International Security Affairs from 1967 to 1969, and included among its members such other former high-ranking defense officials as Herbert York, Roswell Gilpatric, Townsend Hoopes, and Morton Halperin. The Center for Defense Information was headed by a retired navy rear admiral, Gene Larocque, while the Brookings budget analyses were done under the overall direction of Charles Schultze, the director of the Bureau of the Budget in the Johnson administration. The most systematic and detailed alternatives to the administration's defense budget were presented each year by the Brookings Institution in its annual *Setting National Priorities* studies which were inaugurated in the spring of 1970. The low option alternative defense budgets of the Brookings group proposed reductions about 15 percent below the amount recommended by the Pentagon. The reductions, which were offered by Brookings in the FY 1971-1974 period, are contained in Table 26. Had these been accepted, defense spending would have been reduced by an additional $50 billion.

Table 26   Comparison of DOD Budgets and Brookings Low Options, FY 1971 to FY 1974 (in billions of dollars)

| | Fiscal Year | | | | |
	1971	1972	1973	1974	**Total**
DOD	77	79	83	85	324
Brookings					
Low Option	59	69	72	75	275
Difference	18	14	11	10	49
% Reduction	23	17	13	12	15

Sources: Charles Schultze et al., *Setting National Priorities* (Washington, D.C.: Brookings Institution, 1970-1973).

Despite the wide publicity given these alternative budgets, their impact on the final defense budgets was marginal. Whereas some of the counterbudgets were suggesting cuts of up to 30 percent, Congress made reductions in the neighborhood of only 6 percent. Thus, those who wished to reduce defense expenditures more substantially decided to appeal over the head of the legislature directly to the American people in a presidential campaign.

Accordingly, in 1972, individuals such as Warnke, Larocque, and Schultze joined the campaign of Senator George McGovern (D-S.D.), and along with former Secretary of Defense Clarke Clifford were instrumental in persuading the candidate to offer an alternative defense budget to the American people as an integral part of his campaign. McGovern stated that if he were elected president, he would reduce defense spending to $54.8 billion by FY 1975. This was about $30 billion, or 35 percent, less than the level then contemplated by the Nixon administration for that year.

McGovern offered the American public a real choice of the role that it could play in world politics. His defense posture would have guaranteed the physical security of the nation but would have severely limited the ability of the United States to influence the course of events in the international arena.[26] If the American public really wished to have a radically different defense posture, McGovern's alternative program offered it to them. If his plan had been accepted, the whole thrust of post-World War II American foreign policy would have been reversed. A comparison of the force structure proposed by McGovern and the one that actually prevailed in FY 1975 demonstrates the significant choice offered by the Democratic candidate. This comparison is shown in Table 27.

McGovern envisioned a much smaller personnel force. By FY 1975 he intended to reduce the level of military personnel to 1.7 million and cut the level of civilians to under .8 million. This is about 20 percent or 627,000 men below the levels which actually prevailed in 1975. These personnel reductions would have saved about $8.6 billion. In the area of strategic forces, the Democratic candidate would have retained almost the exact number of land-based and sea-based missiles as the Pentagon. However, the senator would have stopped the program of placing multiple independently targeted warheads (MIRVs) on these missiles in January 1973, that is, at the beginning of the new presidential term. Thus, by 1975 only 362 of our strategic missiles would have had MIRV capability. This is 652, or 64 percent, less than the number in the Pentagon's inventory in 1975. McGovern would also have eliminated about 60 percent of our bomber force. Consequently, the number of warheads in the American strategic arsenal would have been just over 4,000 as compared to the 8,500 actually possessed by the Pentagon in 1975. McGovern's

Table 27   Comparison of McGovern Defense Posture with the Pentagon for 1975

Category	McGovern	Pentagon	McGovern Reduction (percentage)	Estimated Savings (in billions)
Personnel				(8.6)
Military	1,735,000	2,129,000	19	
Civilian	761,000	994,000	24	
Total	2,496,000	3,123,000	20	
Strategic Forces				(6.5)
ICBMs	1,000	1,054	5	
SLBMs	656	656	-	
Bombers	200	495	60	
MIRVs	362	1,014	64	
Total Warheads	4,184	8,500	51	
General Purpose				(14.9)
Naval Forces				
Attack Carriers	6	13	54	
Nuclear Submarines	64	64	-	
Escort Ships	130	187	25	
Amphibious Assault	56	65	14	
Support	80	125	36	
Total Ships	336	454	26	
Tactical Air Wings				
Air Force	18	22	22	
Navy	6	14	57	
Marine	2	3	33	
Total	26	39	33	
Land Divisions				
Army	10	13	23	
Marine	2	3	33	
Total	12	16	25	

Source: David Ott, Lawrence Korb et al., *Nixon-McGovern and the Federal Budget* (Washington, D.C.: American Enterprise Institute, 1972).

strategic forces would have cost about $11.5 billion, or $6.5 billion less than the United States spent in 1975.

The Democratic candidate also planned to make significant reductions in DOD's conventional or general purpose forces. Had he been elected, McGovern planned to leave only one naval program unchanged—the nuclear attack submarine program. He proposed to reduce significantly all of the other ship classes by eliminating more than half of the attack carriers, one-quarter of the escort ships, 14 percent of the amphibious assault ships, and 36 percent of the support ships. Overall, the senator hoped to reduce the number of ships by 118, or 26 percent below the planned number. He would have acted similarly with respect to tactical air power and land forces, and he envisioned reducing the number of tactical air wings by one-third, with the greatest number of cuts coming in the area of carrier-based Navy planes. The candidate also argued that this nation could provide for its needs with only twelve divisions of ground combat troops as opposed to the sixteen that it actually possessed in 1975. His general purpose force structure would have cost $14.9 billion less than the Pentagon was spending in 1975.

McGovern's alternative defense posture was criticized in many quarters, even outside the Pentagon. Despite the great number of former high-level defense officials associated with the project, there were glaring errors in its mathematics. One study showed that McGovern could not do what he intended for less than $63.6 billion.[27] Nevertheless, for the first time in the post-World War II period, the American voters were presented in the 1972 campaign with a realistic choice about America's defense posture.

In 1952, the Republicans had accused the Democrats, who were then waging a war in Korea, of being "soft on communism." During the 1960 election, both John Kennedy and Richard Nixon favored a strong national defense. In the 1968 campaign, Richard Nixon accused Lyndon Johnson, who had sent one-half million men to Vietnam, of allowing the United States to become a paper tiger.

The attack by the Nixon administration against the McGovern defense program was coordinated from the Pentagon by its civilian leadership, most notably Secretary of Defense Laird and Comptroller Robert Moot. (The military leadership could not become involved in partisan politics.) Several documents were issued which pointed out reductions which had already been made in the defense posture. The most remarkable of these was a 205-page book with thirty tables and a four-page statistical appendix entitled *The Economics of Defense Spending: A Look at the Realities*.[28] This volume was issued in July 1972 soon after McGovern received the Democratic nomination. It definitely established that most of McGovern's criticisms of the defense budget were primarily myths.

The book focused on eleven of the most significant criticisms commonly made about the size and distribution of the defense budget in 1972 and then systematically pointed out that each of these charges could not stand up to rigorous analysis. In essence, Laird and Moot demonstrated that by 1972 the Pentagon and its leaders were well on their way to meeting the challenges posed by the post-Vietnam environment. The eleven myths that they exploded were:

1. Myth: *The national defense budget continues to grow.*

   Reality: FY 1973 spending will be the lowest, *in real terms*, since FY 1951. None of the real growth in the economy over the past twenty-two years is currently allocated to national defense.

   Since the wartime peak (FY 1968), defense manpower (military, civil service, and defense-related industry) falls by 35 percent, or 2.8 million. Purchases from industry fall by 40 percent, or $22 billion, in constant prices.

2. Myth: *In recent years many additional billions of dollars have been poured into weapons systems and facilities.*

   Reality: Over the past nine years, funds for procurement, research and development, and military construction have increased by only 4 percent, or $900 million. In terms of real buying power, these funds have decreased by 24 percent in the same period.

3. Myth: *The defense budget dominates public spending.*

   Reality: In FY 1973, defense will account for about 20 percent of public spending, about 21 percent of all public employment, and just over 6 percent of the GNP, the lowest shares in more than twenty years.

4. Myth: *The country is operating under a wartime economy; or, defense spending is the root of all economic ills.*

   Reality: We had a war economy in 1945 and in 1953 (Korea), but *not* in recent times.

In constant 1958 prices, defense spending in 1945 was $153 billion; social and economic spending was $34 billion.

Again in constant 1958 prices, social and economic spending will be $145 billion in 1973; defense accounts for $44 billion.

In 1945, total public employment was 19 million of which 78 percent went to defense. In 1973, the total will be 16 million, with 79 percent to *non-defense* purposes.

Since 1961, the economy has created 16 million new jobs while defense employment for all purposes has decreased.

Those who say that defense is dominant are pretending that non-defense public spending does not involve real money or real people.

5. Myth: *Defense is placing an inordinate drain on the nation's research and development resources.*

   Reality: Defense-related R and D is smaller (in real terms) in 1972 than in 1958 or any year since.

6. Myth: *Defense spending is a dominant factor in the balance of payments (BOP) problem.*

   Reality: Defense did play a major role in the past, but not any longer.

               In the FY 1956-1959 era, foreign expenditures by defense were equivalent to 24.4 percent of merchandise imports.

               In FY 1972, defense foreign expenditures have fallen to 9.9 percent of merchandise imports. The $3 billion defense deficit makes up a relatively small part of the $28 billion total deficit.

7. Myth: *Defense has contributed to inflation and BOP problems, causing higher prices and lower productivity in United States industry.*

   Reality: Inflation in the United States has been most severe since 1968, a period when defense programs were being massively cut back.

The aircraft industry—twenty times more dependent on defense than United States industry in general—shows productivity increases nearly double the average and has the best balance of trade record in the economy.

Inflation has been most severe in those industry sectors where the defense input is the smallest, and conversely. For example: the greatest inflation by far (76.4 percent in 1964-1971) is in construction, where defense accounts for less than 1 percent of the business. Five sectors have had above-average inflation, and defense accounts for less than 1 percent of the business in four of them, and 2.7 percent in the fifth.

According to Department of Commerce figures, inflation in state and local government purchases has been greater than in defense purchases.

8. Myth: *Defense takes 60 percent or more of the tax dollar.*

   Reality: In Fy 1973, defense accounts for 31 percent of federal spending and about 20 percent of all public spending, the lowest since before Pearl Harbor. The myth is rationalized by these distortions:

   Adding to the cost of national defense the costs of the federal debt, veterans programs, international programs and space programs.

   Not counting huge amounts of federal taxing and spending which, at $72.5 billion in FY 1973, nearly equal the entire national defense budget.

   Ignoring state and local spending altogether which in FY 1973 amount to $182.5 billion (2.3 times national defense spending) and which come from the same taxpayers, in large part financed through the federal budget.

9. Myth: *The peace dividend has been stolen.*

   Reality: Since the peak of the war in 1968, there have been massive defense cuts which should have resulted in massive spending cuts of about $24 billion. But there is only a $1.5 billion drop in the budget. Why?

> Pay increases to military and civil service personnel account for $16.3 billion.
>
> General inflation on purchased goods and services eats up $6.2 billion.
>
> These add up to $22.5 billion; pay and price increases have offset the massive force reductions. Without these increases, the FY 1973 budget would be $54 billion.

10. Myth: *Defense squanders billions in weapons system "cost overruns."*

   Reality: Alleged "cost overruns" of tens of billions are arrived at by comparing current estimates of all-time (concept to completion of production) costs to very early "planning estimates." Only about half the money referred to in "cost overrun" figures has ever been requested of Congress, much less appropriated or spent. Costs of defense programs increase just as costs in every aspect of our society increase for many valid reasons not associated with waste and mismanagement.

11. Myth: *Defense contractors make exorbitant profits.*

   Reality: The General Accounting Office (GAO) found in a recent study that rates of return for contractors on defense work were 4.3 percent of sales before taxes and 2.3 percent of sales after taxes—significantly lower than on comparable commercial work.

Because there were so many other features which contributed to McGovern's defeat, it is difficult to say to what extent the American people were influenced by the Pentagon's counterattack on his defense program. Nonetheless, the fact that McGovern was forced to revise his alternative defense budget on several occasions, coupled with the magnitude of his defeat, seemed to reflect that in 1972 the American people preferred the adjustments made by DOD to the profound changes suggested by McGovern.[29] This was an indication that the Pentagon was making a successful adjustment to the post-

Vietnam environment. Indeed, beginning in 1975, the year in which the McGovern budget was to take effect, the Pentagon's fortunes began to improve markedly. However, to understand fully the rise of the Pentagon, it is necessary to analyze the leaders who brought it through its darkest days.

Conclusion

From 1969 to 1974 the Pentagon had to adjust to internal and external challenges to its force levels. The internal challenges came from rapid inflation, increased personnel costs, and the high cost of replacing obsolete weapons. The Pentagon responded with Vietnamization and by reducing personnel levels and weapons inventories, instituting the hi-lo mix, adding missions to existing forces, improving its management practices, and reducing overhead costs. The external challenges were posed by Congress and by Senator George McGovern, the presidential challenger in 1972. The Pentagon coped with congressional pressure on the defense budget by exploiting the authority outlay gap and using the supplement. However, the new Congressional Budget Act promises to increase congressional pressure on the Pentagon. The McGovern threat to reduce the defense budget by 43 percent was rejected by the American people. The successful adjustments would not have been possible without good leadership—the civilian and military leaders who directed the affairs of DOD in the post-Vietnam period.

Notes

1. Most of the budgetary figures in this chapter were obtained by analyzing *The Budget of the United States* for the appropriate year. This document is issued each January by the U.S. Government Printing Office, Washington, D.C. Detailed figures on the Pentagon, not available in the budget, were obtained from the Office of the Assistant Secretary of Defense, Comptroller (OASD(C)).

2. In 1978, President Carter's Commission on Military Compensation also recommended overhauling the retirement system.

3. U.S., Congress, House Appropriations Committee, *Hearings on the Defense Budget for FY 1967,* I, p. 280.

4. Richard Nixon, *U.S. Foreign Policy for the 1970's*, February 18, 1970, p. 27.

5. National Security Decision, memorandum 3, printed in John Leacocos, "Kissinger's Apparat," *Foreign Policy*, Winter 1971, p. 25.

6. For an explanation of the Kennedy and Johnson policy, see William Kaufmann, *The McNamara Strategy* (New York: Harper and Row, 1964).

7. George Wilson, "U.S. First Strike Called Conceivable," *Washington Post*, July 2, 1975, p. A1. See also the speech of Secretary Schlesinger to the Overseas Writers Association, Washington, D.C., January 10, 1974.

8. James Schlesinger, *Annual Report of the Secretary of Defense, FY 1975*, March 4, 1974, pp. 3-6.

9. Press Conference, June 24, 1975.

10. U.S. Arms Control and Disarmament Agency, *World Military Expenditures and Arms Trade*, publication 74, 1975, p. 119; Department of State, *U.S. Foreign Military Sales*, July 1975, p. 1.

11. Michael Getler, "Marines to Serve in Germany," *Washington Post*, September 12, 1975, p. 28.

12. Charles Corddry,"Naval Air Pact Is Signed," *Baltimore Sun*, September 29, 1975, p. 1; Robert Ginsburgh, "A New Look at Control of the Seas," *Strategic Review*, Winter 1976, pp. 86-89.

13. Melvin Laird, *Fiscal Year 1972-76 Defense Program and the 1972 Defense Budget*, March 1, 1971, pp. 125-27.

14. Many of those who wished to reduce defense expenditures more substantially were not anti-defense, but pro-social programs. As discussed in Chapter 1, since defense represented about 70 percent of the controllable expenditures in the total federal budget, the only realistic way to obtain more money for social programs was to cut back on defense.

15. *House Report 1406*, 1962, p. 4.

16. *Congressional Record*, March 21, 1962, p. 4309.

17. Prior to FY 1962, the armed services committees played only a minor role in the budget process. Section 412(B) of the Military Construction Act of 1959 brought them into the process by providing that after December 30, 1960, no funds could be appropriated for procurement of aircraft, missiles, or naval vessels without prior authorization. U.S., Statutes at Large, LXXII, 322, Sec. 412.

18. John Finney, "Navy Estimates on F-18 Found $1.6 Billion Short," *New York Times*, July 18, 1975, p. 1.

19. For an excellent analysis of this situation see the letter of Robert Berry, former general counsel of the Department of the Army, *Washington Post*, June 15, 1975, p. A18.

20. The Pentagon has three years to obligate all procurement funds

except those for shipbuilding, for which it has five years. R and D funds must be obligated within two years.

21. Francis Rourke, *Bureaucracy and Foreign Policy* (Baltimore: Johns Hopkins, 1972), p. 27.

22. The Vietnam War years are excluded because the supplemental technique was pursued consciously to mask the real costs of the war.

23. Author's interview with members of the Comptroller's Office, April 1975.

24. Quoted in Nancy Ross, "Budget Adding Jobs Asked by Top House Democrats," *Washington Post*, September 9, 1976, p. B1. For a similar view see (Vice President) Walter Mondale, *The Accountability of Power* (New York: David McKay, 1975), pp. 140-41.

25. "A recent survey shows that a clear majority of the members of the Congressional Budget Committees have historically voted more favorably for social than military programs." Senator Strom Thurmond (R-S.C.), speech to the American Defense Preparedness Association, Washington, D.C., November 11, 1975.

26. The two best sources of McGovern's defense posture are his remarks in the *Congressional Record*, January 24, 1972, pp. 1-5, and his statement before the Subcommittee on Priorities and Economy in Government, Joint Economic Committee, June 16, 1972.

27. David Ott, Lawrence Korb et al., *Nixon-McGovern and the Federal Budget* (Washington, D.C.: American Enterprise Institute, 1972), pp. 35-40.

28. Department of Defense (Comptroller), *The Economics of Defense Spending: A Look at the Realities*, July 1972. See also Melvin Laird, *Final Report to the Congress*, January 1973, pp. 101-4.

29. McGovern's alternative defense budget appeared in print for the first time on pp. 1-5 of the *Congressional Record*, January 24, 1972. A revised version was presented to the Subcommittee on Priorities and Economy in Government of the Joint Economic Committee, June 16, 1972.

CHAPTER 3

A New Type of Secretary of Defense

Introduction

The ability of any large organization to adjust to changing circumstances will depend to a great extent upon its leadership. In the Department of Defense, there are two primary strata of leaders. Civilian control of the military and the department's overall direction are the primary responsibilities of the Secretary of Defense, who is a political appointee of cabinet-level rank. Military leadership is exercised by a five-man committee of career officers known as the Joint Chiefs of Staff (JCS) or the Chiefs. Four of the officers on the JCS gain membership by virtue of being named as head of one of the military services.[1] The fifth member is chairman. He is a career officer and may come from any of the services, but during his tenure he has no service responsibilities.

In the immediate post-Vietnam period, the Pentagon was fortunate to have the right kind of civilian and military leadership, that is, men whose background and style fit the circumstances of the changed environment. Without these high-quality leaders, it is questionable whether DOD could have coped so successfully with the problems besetting it in the late 1960s and early 1970s. Doubtless, other men could have provided leadership that was as good or better. However, those particular men did move the Pentagon in the proper direction. Moreover, their career patterns were markedly different from those of their predecessors. These totally different "prior experiences" may well have been the key variable that allowed the defense leadership to perceive correctly the new environment and to take the measures necessary to cope with it.

The Secretaries of Defense

The first nine secretaries of defense came primarily from the business community.[2] Many people view the Pentagon as the world's largest corporation, and the best preparation for serving as its head was often assumed to be prior high-level business experience. Indeed, three men came directly to DOD from their positions as heads of large corporations. Charles Wilson, who directed DOD from 1953 through 1957, came to Washington from the presidency of General Motors. His successor, Neil McElroy, was president of Proctor and Gamble. Robert McNamara, whose tenure as Secretary of Defense spanned virtually the entire Kennedy and Johnson administrations, was the president of Ford Motor Company when John Kennedy unexpectedly asked him to move from Detroit to Washington.

Three other secretaries of defense came to the Pentagon with extensive backgrounds in high-level finance. The first Secretary of Defense, James Forrestal, had played a major role in building up Dillon, Read, a New York investment house, and had served as its president for two years. Robert Lovett, who headed the Pentagon during the last sixteen months of the Truman administration, was a full partner in the Wall Street banking firm of Brown Brothers, Harriman and a member of the board of directors of several railroads and insurance companies before joining the executive branch. Thomas Gates, the last Secretary of Defense in the Eisenhower period, was an investment banker in Philadelphia when he joined the administration. In addition to their common backgrounds in finance, Forrestal, Lovett, and Gates shared another characteristic. Before being named as Secretary of Defense, all three had served an extensive apprenticeship in the national security bureaucracy. Forrestal had been with the Department of the Navy for seven years before his selection. During that period he served as both Under Secretary and Secretary of the Navy. Lovett was a member of the Roosevelt and Truman administrations for eleven years before being named to head the Pentagon. He had been Assistant Secretary of the Army, Under Secretary of State, and Deputy Secretary of Defense. Gates joined the Eisenhower administration in early 1953 and served as Under Secretary and Secretary of the Navy and as Deputy Secretary of Defense before becoming the Secretary of Defense in late 1959.

Of the remaining three secretaries of defense, two were corporate lawyers with previous experience in the executive branch, and one was a career Army officer. Louis Johnson, who succeeded Forrestal, had his own law firm and had served as Assistant Secretary of War under Roosevelt. Clark Clifford, who headed the Pentagon for the last ten months of the Johnson administration, also headed one of Washington's most prestigious law firms and had served as Truman's legal counsel. General of the Army George C. Marshall, who headed DOD during the first year of the Korean War, was a career officer who had been Army Chief of Staff during World War II and had served as Secretary of State in the immediate post-World War II period.[3]

The Laird Era (1969-1973)

While the first nine secretaries were distinguished men in their own fields, none was a career politician. Not one had ever run for elective office on a national or even a local level. Thus, many were surprised when President-Elect Richard Nixon named Melvin Laird to take over the Pentagon at the most critical period in its twenty-five-year history. Laird had no law, business, or executive experience. In fact, he never held a full-time civilian job in the private sector or the executive branch. However, his long career as a legislator had made him sensitive to popular moods, skilled in the art of compromise, and expert in getting along with people with opposing views.[4]

After graduating from college, Laird went directly into the Navy and served aboard a destroyer in the final stages of the Pacific campaign. When World War II ended, Laird returned home and ran successfully for the seat in the Wisconsin legislature left vacant by his father's unexpected death. When he entered the state legislature in early 1947, Laird was only twenty-three years old, the youngest person ever to serve in that body. He remained for three terms and, in 1952, at the age of twenty-eight, was elected to Congress from Wisconsin's Seventh District. Laird represented that district for the next sixteen years, and had just been reelected for the ninth time when he was unexpectedly nominated to the Nixon cabinet.

Laird did not want to become Secretary of Defense, nor for that matter was he President Nixon's first choice for the post. The President originally wanted to name Senator Henry Jackson (D-Wash.) and enlisted Laird's assistance in recruiting the hawkish Washington senator for his cabinet. Jackson initially accepted the offer, but, under strong pressure from the Democratic leadership, backed out the day before Nixon was scheduled to present his cabinet to the American people via national television. Nixon then pressed the job of heading the Pentagon on Laird.

Four years later, when he voluntarily stepped down, Laird was hailed universally by Pentagon watchers, military leaders, and congressmen as a very effective Secretary of Defense. F. Edward Hebert (D-La.), then Chairman of the House Armed Services Committee, went so far as to call Laird "the finest Secretary of Defense ever."[5] Hebert's sentiments were echoed by most military officers. Rarely had there been such unanimous praise among career officers for a civilian leader. Yet, if the decisions made by Laird during his years in the Pentagon are examined carefully, one would expect to find a great deal of discontent among military leaders and other supporters of a strong national defense. Laird entered the Pentagon when military morale was quite low and during his tenure the military establishment had been reduced by more than one-third, the draft had been discontinued, the size of the weapons inventory had diminished dramatically, spending on investment had declined substantially, and the military was forced to concede failure in Southeast Asia.

All of these actions were necessary if the Pentagon were to adjust to its new environment. Nonetheless, they ran counter to the vested interests of the military, whose morale was already low when Laird took over. Since the Secretary of Defense not only must shape DOD to the demands of the external environment, but must also maintain the morale of the career military, the crucial question is how did Laird accomplish these inherently antimilitary actions and simultaneously maintain the support of the military? The answer lies in his approach. Within the Pentagon he used a leadership style called "participatory management," which made the military feel that they were playing a part in controlling their own destiny. Outside of the department he acted vigorously to prevent others from interfering in those defense matters which he considered the proper domain of DOD.[6]

Participatory Management

The military institution that Laird inherited in 1969 was thoroughly demoralized. In addition to the frustrations caused by the seemingly endless and directionless war in Vietnam and the negative attitude of the American people and the Congress, military men had been treated as second-class citizens by the previous administration. In his nearly eight years at the Pentagon, Secretary of Defense Robert McNamara had virtually excluded the miltary from the decision-making process within the Pentagon. Moreover, he literally derided the military's claim to expertise based upon their experience. The JCS had become so frustrated in its dealings with McNamara that at one point the Chiefs talked about resigning en masse.[7] Only the feeling that their successors would have to face the same problems kept them from taking that step.

McNamara strove to manage the Pentagon almost singlehandedly. In exercising this one-man rule, he relied on two interrelated decision-making tools, the planning-programming-budgeting system (PPBS) and systems analysis (SA). These techniques allowed him to make decisions on a cost-effective basis using quantified data wherever possible. These analyses were performed primarily by the Office of Systems Analysis, which McNamara created and staffed with bright young men from the academic and business worlds, and whom the military disparagingly dubbed "the whiz kids."

McNamara's control over the Pentagon was most evident during the annual budgetary process, where the most important and far-reaching decisions in DOD are made.[8] During the planning phase of the process, the JCS produced a detailed program known as the Joint Strategic Objectives Plan (JSOP). It outlined the threats which jeopardized the security of this nation and recommended the military forces which the Chiefs believed were necessary to counter the threat. To make the JSOP as realistic as possible, the Chiefs continually beseeched McNamara for political and fiscal guidance, but the Secretary refused to provide it. His only advice to the JCS was not to feel bound by any fiscal constraints because this nation could afford whatever was necessary for its defense. As a consequence, the JSOP was totally unrealistic and ignored by McNamara and his associates. Thus the Chiefs were put into the position of having their ideas rejected on military and not fiscal grounds. Moreover, since only the

Secretary knew the final budget figure, the Chiefs could not set priorities.[9]

However, there were some documents produced by the civilians working in systems analysis which became very relevant for the defense budget. While the JCS was working on the JSOP, the civilian analysts were writing a Major Program Memorandum (MPM) for each of the ten program areas in the defense budget.[10] These memoranda summarized the positions of the Office of the Secretary of Defense (OSD) on the major force levels, the rationale for choices among alternatives, and the recommended force levels and funding. Normally, there were huge differences between the JSOP and the MPM. However, rather than trying to reconcile the two, McNamara only asked the military leaders to review the MPM. If the JCS did challenge the positions or the assumptions of the analysts, the Chiefs were nearly always overruled by the Secretary, usually because the military was unfamiliar with the language and nuances of cost-effective analysis and because McNamara refused to make allowances for any input based on experience. On occasion, McNamara would go through the formality of meeting with the Chiefs to discuss their objections but these meetings rarely changed anything. McNamara was not really interested in hearing their opinions; he held the meetings only to find support for his own ideas or attempt to divide the Chiefs on the issues.

The control McNamara exercised over the defense budget process was virtually complete. Each year he made more than seven hundred budgetary decisions himself. Often, these decisions concerned such trivial matters as the color of belt buckles worn by the individual services. Even the powerful Bureau of the Budget and the Congress had little impact on his budgets. For all departments except DOD, the Budget Bureau could make any budgetary changes it wished, but if the bureau wished to alter McNamara's budgets, it had to seek permission from the White House.

Moreover, if the military Chiefs did attempt to go over McNamara's head to the White House, or to make an "end run" to the Congress to challenge one of his decisions, retribution by the Secretary was swift and severe. Within two years after taking over, McNamara had fired all four members of the JCS for publicly challenging his methods and decisions. Even those civilians who sought to support a military position did not last long. The first group of service secretaries appointed by McNamara all resigned within a year. To obtain stability, McNamara was eventually forced to place men from his own staff in those posts. McNamara's men really became vice-presidents of DOD rather than heads of the Army, Navy, or Air Force.[11] This only increased the frustration of the military which, in addition to its other difficulties, had lost its civilian spokesmen.

From his perspective on the House Appropriations Subcommittee, which dealt with defense expenditures, Melvin Laird concluded that McNamara had overcentralized the Pentagon and had given insufficient weight to professional military judgment. Laird also knew that he needed the support of the military leaders if he were to reduce successfully the size of the military establishment. Accordingly, when he became the tenth Secretary of Defense, the Wisconsin legislator instituted a process which he labeled "participatory management." This process dispersed some of his power and gave the military a much larger voice in the decision-making process. It also forced the military leaders to make the tough choices about which areas of the defense budget should be cut. During his term in office, Laird looked primarily to the military services and the Chiefs for the design of the force structure. The civilian systems analysts were limited to evaluating and reviewing the military's proposals. No longer did they put forth independent proposals of their own. Within the budget process, the cornerstone was no longer the Major Program Memorandum drawn up by systems analysis. Rather, the key documents were the Joint Force Memorandum (JFM) drawn up by the JCS and Program Objective Memoranda (POM) drawn up by the individual services.

Moreover, before developing these documents the military received detailed policy and fiscal guidance from the Secretary. The policy guidance told the services in fairly specific terms exactly what would be expected of them—for example, their mission in Europe was to defend West Berlin. The fiscal guidance specified dollar totals for each service in terms of budget authority for five years and an outlay constraint on each service for the upcoming fiscal year. Figure 3 outlines the budgetary process which existed in the Laird era.

The impact on this process made by Laird's policy and fiscal guidance can be seen by comparing the difference between the budget submissions of the individual services and the budget eventually

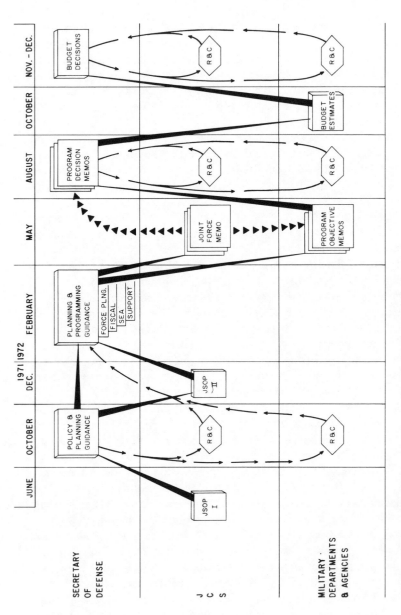

Figure 3 1972 Planning, Programming, Budgeting Cycle.

approved in the McNamara and Laird years. As is indicated in Table 28, in McNamara's eight years in office, his average annual reduction was almost 22 percent. Never once did he have to make a reduction of less than 10 percent in the service budgets. On the other hand, in two of Laird's four years he had to make no reduction at all and his average reduction was just over 4 percent.

Table 28   Reductions by the Secretary of Defense in the Budget Requests of the Military Departments in the McNamara and Laird Periods

Fiscal Year		Percentage Reduction	Period
1963		10.0	
1964		19.7	
1965		28.1	
1966		20.1	McNamara
1967		21.6	
1968		22.9	
1969		24.9	
1970		24.7	
	Average	21.5	
1971		9.1	
1972		0.0	
1973		0.0	Laird
1974		8.2	
	Average	4.3	

Source: Office of the Assistant Secretary of Defense (Comptroller).

The fact that Laird had to make only marginal reductions in the requests of the services improved morale among the military in two ways. First, the military leadership did not have to justify large reductions to their subunits. Second, the fact that their budgets were not substantially modified indicated that they had set the priorities.

Systems analysis was not eliminated from the budgetary process, however. The office did review the JFM of the JCS and the POM of the military services; Laird took the advice of these civilian analysts into account when he made his final budgetary decisions. The difference was that systems analysis no longer originated its own force proposals, as was the case under McNamara. To symbolically emphasize its reduced role, Laird left the post of Assistant Secretary of Defense for Systems Analysis vacant during his first year in office, and eventually downgraded the position of head of systems analysis from the level of assistant secretary to director.

It should also be kept in mind that the military services never wanted to eliminate analysis from the budget process. After the initial shock of the McNamara revolution had worn off, the military leaders recognized that cost benefit or systems analysis added a useful dimension to the defense decision-making process provided it was used as an adjunct to experience and not as a substitute for it. In the view of most military leaders, Laird had actually as well as symbolically placed the Office of Systems Analysis in its proper place in the DOD hierarchy.

Participatory management also meant that the Secretary of Defense would not attempt to exercise control of details in the defense budget. Once he established an annual budget ceiling and "set fences" around specific program categories within the budget, Laird allowed the services wide latitude in structuring the categories. When he had to overrule the services or the JCS regarding the feasibility of certain programs or was forced to eliminate certain desirable weapons systems to conform to fiscal limitations, Laird employed two techniques to make his adverse decisions more palatable.

First, he based his decisions on what he called "net assessment." McNamara had never hesitated to overrule the military leaders on strictly military grounds as he did when he opposed the JCS position on the ABM. The former president of Ford never shied away from pitting his military expertise against that of the uniformed Chiefs. Laird's decisions were based not only on military considerations but also on political, fiscal, and manpower realities; that is, the Secretary made a net assessment of the entire situation. Therefore, when Laird turned down a request from the Navy for a third nuclear carrier in 1971, he did not challenge the military necessity of the carrier, but argued that the economic and political climate would not support a billion-dollar weapons system at that time. Instead, he persuaded the Navy to wait until 1972 when the election-year climate would improve the chances of the program. He used a similar rationale in gaining the support of the JCS for his policy of Vietnamization; that is, the war did not have the necessary political support nor could the Pentagon afford the costs if it wished to modernize its weapon systems while living within rigid fiscal constraints.

Second, the Secretary allowed the military to appeal his decisions whenever and wherever they wished. In fact, he encouraged members of the JCS to take their case to officials in the OMB, the Secretary of the Treasury, the White House itself, or the Congress.[12] The only restriction he placed upon them was that they present their case on its merits and not frame their argument at the expense of another service.

On occasion, the Chiefs were able to persuade other officials in the executive branch to overrule the Secretary; in late 1971, they convinced the President to provide an additional $2 billion for the FY 1972 defense budget.[13] Even when the military was successful in overturning Laird's decisions, he never exacted any retribution. The tenure of all the members of the JCS reached its apex under Laird. For the first time in the history of DOD, all of the Chiefs completed full four-year terms. Tenure of the service secretaries also increased markedly.

Similarly, when Laird met with the JCS to discuss their differences, he came with an open mind and was receptive to arguments based upon their military experience. He often allowed the military to undertake development of certain systems whose cost-benefit rationale may have been somewhat dubious but whose symbolic importance was quite high. For example, the manned strategic bomber is essential to the organizational essence of the Air Force. Indeed, it was the development of the weapon system that led to separating the Air Force from the Army. McNamara repeatedly turned down Air Force requests to undertake the development of a new manned bomber to replace the aging B-52 because its cost effectiveness could not be demonstrated to his satisfaction. Laird, however, recognized the symbolic importance of the manned bomber and allowed the Air Force to develop and build a small number of these planes.

Participatory management and related techniques such as net assessment helped restore the morale of the officer corps in an era of retrenchment for the military. However, in the post-1968 period, it was not sufficient merely to restore the prerogatives of the military within the Pentagon; steps had to be taken to prevent other groups within the federal government from undermining military morale from without. In this area Laird also excelled.

Protection from the Outside

During the McNamara years, the undermining of military prerogatives came from the Secretary himself. After 1969, however, the threat to overwhelm and exclude the military from the national security decision-making process came primarily from Henry Kissinger. As the Executive Assistant for National Security Affairs, the former Harvard professor sought to dominate the entire national security decision-making apparatus by controlling the NSC organization and process. One of the subcommittees of the NSC, established by Kissinger, was the Defense Program Review Committee (DPRC). This group, which was chaired by Kissinger, and had representatives from the State and Defense departments, the OMB, the CIA, and the Council of Economic Advisors, was given the task of assessing the political, economic, and social consequences resulting from changes in the levels of defense spending, budgeting, and force levels. The DPRC was created in October 1969 and reviewed the FY 1970 defense budget in December of that same year. At this late date in the budget process, Kissinger was not able to have much of an impact on the FY 1971 budget. Therefore, he proposed that beginning with the next fiscal year, the DPRC become involved much earlier in the budget cycle, and scheduled a meeting for March 1970. Kissinger wanted his staff to participate in the production of the Pentagon's planning and programming documents. Laird, however, objected to what he felt was an intrusion into his purview and was unwilling to allow the NSC or its staff members to become involved in the early stages of the defense budget process. He claimed that their proper role was to review the budget which he and his Chiefs produced. Laird feared that Kissinger and his staff, many of whom were alumni of McNamara's systems analysis office, would take the initiative in the defense budget process. Thus, the military would be reduced to the same position that they had held under McNamara, that is, commentators rather than initiators.

However, Laird did not wish to confront Kissinger directly. Instead, the Secretary of Defense simply outmaneuvered him. First,

Laird had the March meeting postponed until April. He then submitted documents for the April meeting that were so confusing that the meeting had to be delayed for three months. Finally, the Secretary had the July meeting postponed until August. By this time, most of the major issues in the defense budget had been solved and President Nixon had been briefed on the budget by the JCS.[14]

Not only was Laird able to keep the DPRC out of the essential phases of the budget process, he turned the DPRC into a positive force in his efforts to improve morale within the Pentagon. Laird encouraged the military leaders to use the DPRC as a court of appeals for weapon systems which he had to reject to stay within rigid budgetary limits. It was through appeals to groups such as the DPRC that the Navy was able to obtain funds for Trident. Kissinger eventually saw the futility of trying to use the DPRC to take control of DOD and had the panel reorganized under the chairmanship of the Secretary of Defense and renamed the Defense Review Panel.

In a similar manner, Laird saw to it that military input into operational or crisis situations was institutionalized. Under the Johnson administration, major operational military decisions for the conduct of the war in Vietnam were usually made at the "Tuesday Luncheons" attended for the most part only by the President, the Secretary of State, the Secretary of Defense, and the Executive Assistant for National Security Affairs. A military officer was not included in these forums until the latter stages of the Johnson administration when the President's war policies came under fire and the Chairman of the JCS was added to the group primarily to bring legitimacy to its decisions. Military leaders were also excluded from the decision-making process in other crisis situations in the McNamara years. For example, no member of the JCS or other military official was invited to the White House on April 28, 1965, when the decision was made to commit troops to the Dominican Republic.[15]

Laird recognized that since Kissinger had a tendency to exclude others from the decision-making process, a similar situation could easily occur in the Nixon administration. Therefore, after the first crisis of the Nixon administration, that is, the shooting down of an EC-121 aircraft by the North Koreans in April 1969, Laird proposed that an appendage of the NSC be created to handle similar situations. Nixon approved, and the resulting Washington Special Action

Group (WASAG) handled all of the subsequent crises of the Nixon years. Since one of its members was the Chairman of the JCS, this guaranteed military input into future crisis situations.[16] Figure 4 outlines the NSC system in the Kissinger era.

During the immediate post-Vietnam period, DOD also was placed under siege by Congress. The legislators demanded a large volume of information about Pentagon operations and spent nearly a year scrutinizing every aspect of the defense budget; they also made an unprecedented number of changes in the DOD budget and placed a great many restrictions on DOD operations. Yet during Laird's tenure, DOD never lost a critical vote. Laird was able to maintain all the essential weapons system development programs, while at the same time he allowed Congress to make substantial reductions in the defense budget through the use of the authority/outlay differential. This technique was developed by Laird, who was skilled in the intricacies of the legislative process and aware of the intense public pressures on Congress to make reductions in the defense budget. In fact, during the budget season, Laird turned over the operation of the Pentagon to David Packard, his deputy, so that he could roam the halls of Congress making his case and directing congressional reductions to the right places.

The Secretary also made skillful use of other political ploys to maintain the essentials of his defense program with a hostile Congress. For example, in 1972, he refused to endorse the SALT I agreements unless Congress first approved such major, but controversial new programs as the B-1, the F-14, the F-15, the CV-70, and Trident. Then he arranged to have the Congress vote on the defense budget before it took up the SALT agreement.

Finally it should be noted that Laird kept the Pentagon out of the Watergate affair by refusing to allow DOD to cooperate with David Young and G. Gordon Liddy, of the infamous White House plumbers. Laird told these White House minions that as a cabinet officer he took orders only from the President. The military's image had already been tarnished by some of the less savory aspects of Vietnam, for example, My Lai, the secret bombings of Cambodia, and the unauthorized bombing of North Vietnam. Involvement in Watergate might have completely destroyed its standing with the American people. As it turned out, the military served as a pillar of

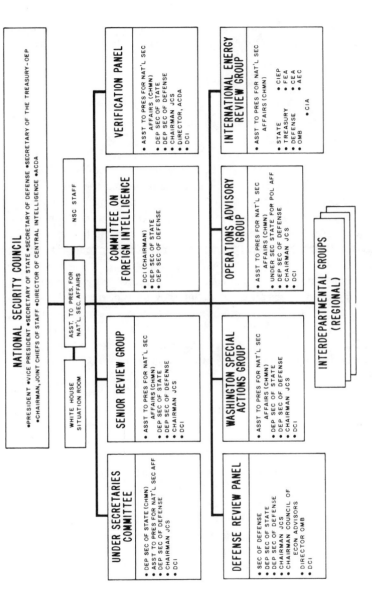

Figure 4 The National Security Council System in the Kissinger Era.

stability during the dark days of Watergate, and escaped the problems that befell such other federal agencies as the CIA and the FBI.

The Schlesinger Period (1973-1975)

Restoring morale within the Pentagon and insulating the department from outside threats accomplished only part of the job of helping the Pentagon to adjust to the realities of the post-Vietnam era. The DOD still needed a convincing rationale for the maintenance of a large military establishment in an era of détente and in a period in which the United States had eschewed the role of world policeman. Laird was either unable or unwilling to articulate a sophisticated justification for the American military. Instead, his policy assumptions were usually couched in glib catchy phrases such as "realistic deterrence," "net assessment," and "total force"; the standard by which he measured United States forces was 1964, the last pre-Vietnam year. These slogans may have bought time for the Pentagon to adjust internally, but they did not deal with the new realities of the domestic and international arenas. The post-Vietnam period was totally different than 1964 when this nation was still "willing to go anywhere, pay any price and bear any burden" to protect freedom. Cold War rhetoric could no longer be used to justify a large defense force.

Fortunately for the military establishment, Laird's successor in the Pentagon was a man who could articulate military strategy as well as anyone in this nation. Like Laird, James R. Schlesinger was not Richard Nixon's first choice for the post of Secretary of Defense. When Laird resigned from DOD in early 1973, he was succeeded initially by Elliot Richardson, who had been serving as the Secretary of HEW. Richardson had barely taken office in the Pentagon when the burgeoning Watergate scandal led to the resignation of Attorney General Richard Kleindienst. Nixon was then forced to switch Richardson to Justice and move Schlesinger from the CIA to DOD.

The President was not totally enthusiastic about either of these appointments, but, in the spring of 1973, Richardson and Schlesinger were among the few people on the Nixon team who could still be confirmed by the Congress.

Unlike his predecessors, Schlesinger did not come to the Pentagon from the worlds of business, law, or politics. The twelfth Secretary of Defense was an economics professor.[17] He received both his undergraduate and graduate education in economics at Harvard, and had spent three years on the faculty at Cambridge specializing in money and banking. In the late 1950s, Schlesinger took a job at the University of Virginia and shifted the focus of his research to the economic aspects of defense policy. After publishing *The Political Economy of National Defense*, he was recruited by the Rand Corporation, the West Coast "think tank" which specialized in defense analysis, to head up their strategic studies section. While at Rand, he came to the attention of the Washington community with his perceptive criticisms of the way in which Secretary of Defense Robert McNamara was employing systems analysis within the Pentagon. In testimony before Henry Jackson's Committee on Government Operations, Dr. Schlesinger argued that the uses of analysis had been oversold and that, in claiming that politics had been replaced by scientific due process, the Pentagon officials were either fools or liars.[18]

In 1969, Schlesinger, a lifelong Republican, joined the Nixon administration as head of the Bureau of the Budget's National Security Branch. In that position he was responsible for prodding the Navy into scrapping several hundred of its older ships and shifting the funds into new construction. During his time at the Bureau of the Budget, he also killed such Pentagon white elephants as the Air Force's Manned Orbiting Laboratory project and the Navy's antisubmarine warfare carrier program, that is, the hunter-killer groups which were no longer capable of coping with nuclear submarines. After two years with the Bureau of the Budget, he became the first nonscientist to be appointed head of the Atomic Energy Commission (AEC). In his year at AEC, Schlesinger aroused the ire of businessmen, but won the support of Congress and the public by shifting the focus of the agency from a concern for the profits of industry to a concern for the environment. He achieved nationwide publicity and came to the attention of President Nixon by taking his wife and several of his children to the site of a nuclear test in Amchitka, Alaska, to demonstrate that the underground explosion of a nuclear warhead was a safe exercise. In 1972, President Nixon selected

Schlesinger to succeed Richard Helms as Director of Central Intelligence. Although he headed the CIA for a comparatively brief period, Schlesinger left his imprint on the agency. He forcibly retired 7 percent of the agency's 18,000 employees and made the CIA describe fully its role in the Ellsberg episode.

When Richardson became Attorney General, Richard Nixon initially offered the post of Secretary of Defense to David Packard, the millionaire Chairman of the Board of Hewlitt-Packard, who had served as Deputy Secretary of Defense under Melvin Laird. Packard turned down the President's offer because he did not wish to sell his stock in his electronics company. The President then turned to Schlesinger. For the purpose of helping the Pentagon adjust to its new environment, it turned out that putting a "professor into the Pentagon" was one of Nixon's better ideas.

When he took over the Pentagon in April 1973, James Schlesinger was only forty-four years old. This made him the youngest Secretary of Defense and the first with no prior military experience. His comparative youth, his lack of military background, and his iconoclastic actions at AEC and CIA concerned some military officers. They feared that he might be another "McNamara-style whiz kid." However, Schlesinger quickly gained their confidence by his ability to articulate a convincing rationale for American strategic and conventional forces in the post-Vietnam era, and eventually became one of the most revered men to head the Pentagon.[19] When President Ford found it necessary to fire Schlesinger two and one-half years later, the loudest protests came from the military leadership.

A New Strategic Nuclear Policy

Since the end of World War II, the cornerstone of this nation's strategic nuclear policy had been the deterrence of nuclear war by assured destruction. The United States attempted to develop and maintain second-strike capability, that is, the ability to withstand a full-scale, well-coordinated surprise attack and then to launch a massive retaliatory strike which would destroy so great a percentage of the population and industry of a potential enemy that even an irrational and desperate leader would be deterred or stopped from initiating a nuclear attack. Against our major rival, the Soviet Union,

American strategists calculated the levels of assured destruction at between one-fifth and one-fourth of the Soviet population and at half of her industrial capacity. After these levels of destruction had been reached, the effectiveness of additional attacks would rapidly decrease; all the worthwhile targets would have been destroyed. By 1967, when it had developed a triad force of 1,054 ICBMs, 656 SLBMs, and about 500 long-range bombers, American planners felt that they had generated a sufficient quantity and variety of delivery systems to maintain an assured destruction capability against the Soviet Union and other potential enemies for the foreseeable future.[20] In fact, the United States possessed more than assured destruction. By the mid-1960s it had overkill capability. Its strategic forces had the capacity to destroy the Soviet Union at least five times over.   *205561*

With the signing of the SALT Agreements in 1972, most analysts felt that the doctrine of assured destruction had been codified and legitimized by the United States and the Soviet Union. The SALT I Agreements initially limited each side to two ABM sites and within a year reduced the number to one. The agreements also set upper limits on the numbers of offensive launchers that both parties could construct. Thus, both the United States and the USSR apparently guaranteed that there would be mutual assured destruction capability on each side of the Atlantic.

Since the United States already possessed an overkill capability, there were strong pressures on DOD to cut back or at least hold its strategic offensive forces at their SALT I level. In fact, DOD had reduced its strategic expenditures by 26 percent in real terms between FY 1971 and FY 1974. However, shortly after taking office, Schlesinger announced that not only would the Pentagon not continue to reduce its strategic expenditures, but it would increase them by at least 10 percent annually so that the yield, accuracy, and range of our strategic missile forces could be improved. To justify this new direction in our strategic policy, Schlesinger used three sophisticated arguments.

First, the greater throw weight of Soviet strategic missile forces could enable them to gain a significant military advantage over this nation. In the SALT I Agreements the United States had accepted an inferior position in the throw weight or lifting capacity of its missile force because of its large advantage in numbers of warheads. However, its lead in warheads was a result of its headstart in MIRV technology. Once the USSR mastered MIRV, the greater lifting capacity of its missiles would allow it to place several warheads on each missile.[21] The defense secretary did not argue that the Soviets would use this advantage to launch a preemptive or successful first strike against the United States. Rather, he felt that the Russians might attempt to use their military advantage for political purposes. He feared that they might try to blackmail this country, or, more probably, our allies. Since in contemporary international politics perception can be more important than reality, the Soviet superiority could be viewed by others as meaningful. To those who viewed his arguments with skepticism, Schlesinger pointed to the way in which many of our European allies and Japan caved in to pressure from the Arabs in the fall of 1973.

The second argument for altering our policy was that in Schlesinger's opinon assured destruction by massive retaliation was too clumsy a policy upon which to base our entire nuclear strategy. The United States needed more choices than simply the option of an all-out attack on the enemy's population or industry, a countervalue attack. This nation ought to develop a capacity to launch a limited or surgical nuclear attack against such military targets as missile silos or airfields. This strategy was known as counterforce or flexible response.

The Secretary argued that the United States needed to develop this capability for four reasons. First, massive retaliation was unacceptable because it could violate the moral principle of proportionality. For example, in the event of a limited counterforce attack against an American military installation, with relatively few civilian casualties, would an American President be justified in ordering the mass slaughter of enemy civilians? Second, massive retaliation might be counterproductive. A President who ordered the mass destruction of enemy civilians would be faced with the certainty that such a move would be followed in turn by mass slaughter of Americans. Third, in light of the fact that massive retaliation might be viewed as immoral and counterproductive, was it a credible deterrent to anything but an all-out countervalue attack against the United States? Since the USSR already had a counterforce capability, how else could the

United States deter the Soviets from a limited attack except by developing its own flexible response capacity? Fourth, a well-developed, refined, and thus credible counterforce capability could serve as a deterrent against conventional attacks in such places as Western Europe and Korea. As was discussed in Chapter 2, this could justify the decrease in our conventional forces in those areas.

The third argument for revising our strategic policy was that the previous levels of assured destruction were now considered too low. In Schlesinger's view, the McNamara concept was now outmoded; it was no longer sufficient to have the capability to destroy between one-fifth and one-fourth of the Soviet population and half of its industrial capacity.[22] In light of Soviet advances in civil defense, the growth and diversification of the Soviet economy, and Soviet efforts to disperse and protect vital industries, a new measure of assured destruction was needed. Henceforth, the United States strategic nuclear forces had to be configured to prevent the Soviet Union from ever recovering militarily, politically, and economically. This was a much more demanding task than simply wiping out a certain percentage of the Soviet population and industry. The McNamara concept could be implemented by delivering only 400 one-megaton equivalents for a retaliatory strike.[23] Adoption of the Schlesinger strategy meant that approximately 8,500 warheads would be required for adequate target coverage.[24]

Schlesinger's arguments had to be quite cogent because pressure against his new strategic policy came not only from the intellectual community and Congress but from within the administration in the person of Henry Kissinger who by 1973 held the dual positions of Secretary of State and Assistant for National Security Affairs.[25] Kissinger, who was anxious to put a cap on the arms race, felt that our strategic forces were adequate and that new American initiatives would alarm the Soviets and hinder future negotiations. Nonetheless, Schlesinger's arguments prevailed within the administration and before the Congress, and DOD received funds for increasing the accuracy and yield of its land- and sea-based missiles, developing terminal guidance, and embarking on a cruise missile program. Just as Melvin Laird had kept Kissinger from dominating the defense budget, Schlesinger kept the Secretary of State from setting strategic nuclear policy. Kissinger apparently became so frustrated at Schlesinger's success that in the summer of 1974 at a press conference in Moscow he declared that no major arms agreements could be achieved until both the United States and the Soviet Union convinced their military establishments of the benefits of restraint.[26]

A Rationale for Conventional Forces

Strategic forces, while quite dangerous, are comparatively inexpensive. In FY 1975, the strategic forces program accounted for $7.2 billion, or only 8.2 percent of the total defense budget. The bulk of the defense budget goes to paying, training, equipping, and maintaining our general purpose or conventional forces. Between 1968 and 1974, the share of the defense budget devoted to general purpose forces had decreased by more than 20 percent and spending on these forces during that period declined by 40 percent in real terms. Schlesinger argued that even in the era of détente, there were five compelling and interrelated reasons why this trend had to be reversed.

First, while our conventional capabilities have been decreasing, the Soviet Union's has been rapidly increasing. In 1968, both the United States and the USSR had approximately 3.4 million men under arms. By 1974, this nation's active forces had declined to about 2 million while the Russian forces had increased to over 4 million. While the number of surface combatants in the U.S. Navy was declining by almost 50 percent, the Soviet Navy was growing in strength. Soviet production of such equipment as tanks, helicopters, tactical aircraft, submarines, and surface ships was about three times greater than that of the United States.

Second, the decrease in our conventional capability vis-à-vis the Soviets lowered the nuclear threshold. If there were to be a conventional attack in Europe, the comparatively weak Allied forces might have to use nuclear weapons to prevent defeat. Crossing the nuclear threshold could unleash mass destruction around the globe. To those who criticized his nuclear policy as making nuclear wars more likely, Schlesinger countered that the best safeguard was to increase the capability of our non-nuclear or conventional forces.

Third, without an adequate conventional capability, this nation could not play a significant role in world affairs. Whether we liked it or not, the Secretary argued, historical circumstances had made the

United States the leader of the non-Communist world. Even in the era of détente, the role of military force is still important in the international arena. If we abandon our responsibilities for the security of the Western world, then we allow others to make the choices that could affect our future. In the mid-1970s, the United States had about $100 billion in investments around the world. Moreover, it was totally dependent on other parts of the globe for about twenty vital raw materials, and conducted $250 billion in trade annually.

Safeguarding these investments and maintaining access to raw materials is critical. Without adequate conventional military power across the entire spectrum of violence, the United States could easily jeopardize its ability to maintain its standard of living. Schlesinger defined this logical relationship between America's military might and its political role in the world when he warned this country in the spring of 1975:

Today in contrast to the situation that existed before 1945 there is no acceptable alternative to deep and steady American support of, and participation in, the security of other free states. The only alternatives are either Finlandization or Polandization, depending upon whether one happens to be an optimist or pessimist. Such an outcome might be tolerable to the relatively few advocates of Little America, it would be wholly intolerable to everybody else.[27]

Fourth, the surest way to continue to have détente with the Soviet Union is to possess a strong defense posture. History has demonstrated that the Soviets respond to those who deal from a position of strength. In Schlesinger's view, "Detente without defense is delusion."

Fifth, because of the failure of our policy in Southeast Asia, the credibility of this nation to act decisively to protect its interests is suspect. Allowing our conventional capabilities to decline could easily be taken as an indication that the United States no longer has the will to honor its commitments.

Schlesinger's arguments also prevailed in the conventional area. The amount of funds and the portion of the budget devoted to conventional forces began to increase in FY 1975. In that year spending for general purpose forces went above the level of FY 1970 for the first time. For FY 1976, the general purpose forces received $35.9 billion, or 34.3 percent, of the DOD budget, an increase of $10.2 billion. This was 40 percent above the post-1968 low point of $25.7 billion. These additional funds allowed the Pentagon to halt the downward trend in such critical conventional areas as the number of ships, divisions, and tactical aircraft.

The Demise of Schlesinger

Despite his success in increasing the strategic and conventional capabilities of our armed forces and in halting the downward trend in defense spending, Schlesinger was still not content. He wished to see a large real increase in the defense budget over the remainder of the decade. The fact that the Soviets were outspending us by 50 percent in the investment area alarmed him greatly. In the view of some, Schlesinger pictured himself as a modern-day Churchill, as one of the few people whose position and sense of history stood between the decaying West and the Communist hordes to the East.[28] Consequently, in the fall of 1975 when Congress reduced his FY 1976 budget by approximately $7.5 billion, Schlesinger lashed out at the lawmakers, denouncing the cuts as savage and arbitrary, and demanded that they restore at least $2.6 billion. Moreover, when President Ford, in an attempt to court favor with fiscal conservatives by "holding the line" on the federal budget, ordered the Pentagon to reduce the projected level of defense spending for FY 1977 by an additional $7 billion, Schlesinger protested to the Chief Executive that cuts of that magnitude risked a serious weakening of the American military posture. The Secretary also let it be known that if the President persisted in that course of action he might be forced to resign.

Although President Ford fired Schlesinger the day after the Secretary said he could not support the $7 billion reduction, this was not the only reason for Schlesinger's dismissal after serving only two and one-half years in office. The President had at least four other reasons for taking this drastic step. First, he was not comfortable with the way in which Schlesinger interacted with him or the Congress. The former college professor had the arrogant habit of "lecturing down" to both the President and the Congress. As one Pentagon correspondent noted, "He [Schlesinger] could be extremely arrogant, delighting in overwhelming an opponent with the force of his own intellect. He could be unpleasant and unfeeling in his personal relationships."[29] Another commented that "Schlesinger's sardonic humor did not entrance the President."[30]

Second, President Ford was unhappy with Schlesinger's repeated public dissent from the administration's positions in such areas as strategic arms limitation and the Middle East. In the strategic arms limitations talks between the United States and the Soviet Union, Schlesinger had insisted that the new Soviet bomber, the Backfire, be counted against the ceilings on strategic delivery vehicles and that American cruise missiles be excluded. The President and Secretary of State Kissinger were attempting to stake out a compromise position on these two weapons systems. In firing Schlesinger, the President apparently wished to signal Moscow that the United States was ready to break the deadlock in the strategic arms talks.[31] In a certain sense Schlesinger became the SALT talks' first human bargaining chip.[32]

In September 1975, Kissinger had secured a partial Israeli withdrawal from occupied Egyptian territory in the Sinai Peninsula by promising (among other things) to supply Pershing missiles to the Jewish state. Schlesinger claimed that he was not consulted about supplying the missile to the Israelis and that he opposed taking Pershings from our armed forces. American forces in Europe were still seriously short of equipment because of material shipped to Israel during the October 1973 war.[33] Upon hearing Schlesinger's remarks, Kissinger charged publicly that the Pentagon knew of Israel's interest in the Pershings since August and accused defense officials of making statements in the press that they had never raised within the government.[34] In a speech in Omaha, Nebraska, on October 1, 1975, the President openly backed Kissinger's version and publicly chided his Secretary of Defense. Ford denied Schlesinger's assertion that the Pentagon had not been told of the plan to supply the Pershing missiles as an integral part of the agreement for partial withdrawal from occuped Egyptian territory on the Sinai Peninsula. According to President Ford, "The Pentagon had the shopping list."[35]

Third, the President was unhappy with the way that Schlesinger was running the Pentagon. In an October 10, 1975, news conference, Ford issued a sharp critique of waste in the Pentagon. He declared,

"They can manage the Defense Department better. We can be harder bargainers with weapons suppliers. I think we can cut out some of the frills in the military, frills that I don't like, that have been there just by tradition. I think we can cut them all out."[36] While the President's critique may have been overstated, the fact was that Schlesinger spent very little time on such areas. He preferred to focus on policy issues. In addition, Ford felt that during the *Mayaguez* incident, Schlesinger lost control of events. According to the President, Schlesinger could not explain why two presidentially mandated bombing strikes were not carried out.

Fourth, the President wished to place one of his most trusted associates, Donald Rumsfeld, in a key post within his administration. The Ford-Rumsfeld relationship dated to 1965 when then Congressman Donald Rumsfeld (R-Ill.) helped Gerald Ford (R-Mich.) unseat Congressman Charles Halleck (R-Ind.) as Minority Leader of the House of Representatives. Their relationship grew when Rumsfeld helped Ford reorganize the White House staff after President Nixon's resignation.

Although the Pentagon lost one of its most articulate leaders when Schlesinger was dismissed, the firing did bring some immediate benefits to the military establishment. Ford's abrupt dismissal of Schlesinger along with CIA Director William Colby was referred to by many as the "Sunday Night Massacre." Many Congressmen and several members of the foreign policy elite were outraged. Schlesinger was transformed into an instant hero and his ideas gained new credibility. He was in great demand to testify before Congress and as a public speaker. On November 6, 1975, in an unprecedented action, a bipartisan group of 108 House members sent Schlesinger a letter in which they stated that they believed he ought to have remained as Secretary of Defense.[37] The American public was jolted into thinking more seriously about the threat posed by the Soviet Union.[38] Public pressure forced President Ford to back away from his threatened reduction of $7 billion in the FY 1977 defense budget and prevented the Ford administration from concluding a strategic arms agreement on terms that the Pentagon hierarchy considered unfavorable. The proposed agreement, which Secretary of State Kissinger had negotiated in late 1975, had three features that DOD opposed: The Soviet Backfire bomber would not be considered as a strategic weapon; U.S. B-52s armed with cruise missiles would be counted as multiple-warhead weapons; and long-range cruise missiles would be banned from submarines.[39]

Rumsfeld's Tenure (1975-1976)

The replacement of Schlesinger as Secretary of Defense by Donald Rumsfeld did not leave the Pentagon without a sympathetic or effective leader. Rumsfeld's views on defense were virtually identical to those of Schlesinger. As the thirteenth Secretary of Defense stated in his confirmation remarks, "I don't know of any policy differences I have with James Schlesinger." Then Rumsfeld went on to specifically endorse Schlesinger's changes in nuclear strategy and stressed that he, like Schlesinger, believed that there must be continued real growth in the level of defense spending.[40] Moreover, Rumsfeld was well qualified to head DOD. Although President Ford stated somewhat lamely that Rumsfeld was a good choice for Secretary of Defense because he was a former naval aviator, the fact was that Rumsfeld had a great many more qualifications for the post. Indeed, while Rumsfeld may not have had all the same attributes as Schlesinger, he was more prepared to be Secretary of Defense than most of his predecessors.

Rumsfeld was the first Secretary of Defense to have broad experience in both the legislative and executive branches of government. He was elected to the House of Representatives in 1960, at the age of twenty-nine, and was a member of the Lower House for eight years. From 1968 through 1975, Rumsfeld served in a wide variety of cabinet-level assignments in the executive branch. During Nixon's tenure, he was head of the Office of Economic Opportunity, director of the Cost of Living Council, and ambassador to NATO. When Ford assumed the presidency, he selected Rumsfeld to be the White House Chief of Staff. In addition to his wide background in the two branches of the federal government, Rumsfeld had two other attributes not possessed by Schlesinger. First, he had the President's complete trust and confidence and virtually unlimited access to him. As Ford stated so plainly at his press conference announcing the appointment, "Rumsfeld is my guy." Second, Rumsfeld had a long and close association with the uniformed military. Following his four years of active service with the Navy, he had remained an active member of the Naval Reserve and at the time of his appointment held the rank of captain.

During his short time in the Pentagon, Rumsfeld used his background and prior experience to become an effective Secretary of Defense and accomplished some things that Schlesinger could not. In fact, William Clements, Deputy Secretary of Defense for both Schlesinger and Rumsfeld, considers Rumsfeld the better Secretary.[41] Rumsfeld's primary accomplishments in office may be broken down into three categories. First, through his access to the Oval Office, he was able to convince President Ford to lay the foundation for a program that would have raised the defense budget by about 4 percent per year in real terms, that is, 4 percent above the rate of inflation, during the latter half of the decade of the 1970s. The Ford-Rumsfeld program would have raised defense spending from $87 billion in FY 1975 to $145 billion by FY 1980.[42]

Second, Rumsfeld used his contacts on the Hill to convince the congressional leadership that it should not continue to make such large reductions in the annual defense budget. As a result, the defense budget presented to the Congress by Rumsfeld in January 1976 was cut by only 2.4 percent, the smallest reduction in more than a decade.

Third, using his managerial experience he dealt effectively with the scandal that erupted when it was revealed that some high-ranking defense officers had accepted gratuities from defense contractors. Although the indiscretions had taken place before he took office, Rumsfeld issued letters of reprimand to several flag officers and fined the director of Defense Research and Engineering several thousand dollars for accepting trips from North American Rockwell. In addition, he promulgated a revised standards of conduct directive which outlined constraints on the relationships between DOD's employees and defense contractors.[43] Rumsfeld's swift action defused the scandal and prevented it from impeding the Pentagon's recovery.

Conclusion

Melvin Laird, James Schlesinger, and Donald Rumsfeld were men with backgrounds very different from the first five secretaries of defense. Each used his particular blend of talents and skills gained from prior experiences to help DOD deal with its new environment. However, these men could not do it alone. Each was assisted by a unique group of competent military leaders who also differed from their predecessors, men who served on the nation's highest military tribunal, the Joint Chiefs of Staff.

Notes

1. Technically, until 1978 the Commandant of the Marine Corps was not a member of the JCS. According to a law passed in 1952, he was supposed to attend only those meetings of the JCS during which matters pertaining to the Marine Corps were discussed. However, in reality he was the fourth service chief and attended and voted at all meetings of the JCS.

2. The best source of the backgrounds of the first eight secretaries of defense is C. W. Borklund, *Men of the Pentagon* (New York: Praeger, 1966). Other information can be gathered from such usual sources as *Current Biography* and *Who's Who in America*.

3. In the early days of the Kennedy era, Laird argued with Adam Yarmolinsky, then a principal Deputy Assistant Secretary of Defense, and Senator Henry Jackson (D-Wash.) that public opinion would never support sending Americans to fight in Vietnam. President Nixon states that he undertook Vietnamization largely on the basis of Laird's enthusiastic advocacy. Richard Nixon, *The Memoirs of Richard Nixon* (New York: Grosset and Dunlap, 1978), p. 393.

4. For an excellent analysis of Laird's background, see Nick Thimmesch, "The Back-Room Master in Waiting," *Washington Post/Potomac*, May 5, 1974, pp. 10-38.

5. *Washington Post*, January 9, 1973, p. A1.

6. The best source of Laird's methods is his *Final Report to the Congress*, January 8, 1973. See also *The Annual Reports of the Secretary of Defense for FY 1972 and FY 1973*. Additional information was obtained from interviews with DOD officials.

7. Townsend Hoopes, *The Limits of Intervention* (New York: David McKay, 1968), p. 90.

8. The best source on the budgetary process under McNamara is Alain Enthoven and K. Wayne Smith, *How Much Is Enough* (New York: Harper and Row, 1971).

9. For a complete examination of the role of the JCS in the defense budget process, see Chapter 3 in my *The Joint Chiefs of Staff: The First Twenty-five Years* (Bloomington: Indiana University Press, 1976).

10. These documents were also known as Draft Presidential Memoranda (DPM).

11. For a description of the role of the service secretary in the McNamara era, see Eugene Zuckert, "The Service Secretary: Has He a Useful Role?" *Foreign Affairs*, April 1966, pp. 458-79.

12. Press conference of the Secretary of Defense, August 14, 1971.

13. Morton Halperin, *Bureaucratic Politics and Foreign Policy* (Washington, D.C.: Brookings Institution, 1974), p. 203.

14. For an excellent analysis of how Laird outmaneuvered Kissinger on the DPRC, see Elmo Zumwalt, *On Watch* (New York: Quadrangle, 1976), pp. 335-36.

15. Lyndon Johnson, *The Vantage Point* (New York: Holt, Rhinehart and Winston, 1971), p. 199.

16. Marvin Kalb and Bernard Kalb, *Kissinger* (Boston: Little, Brown, 1974), p. 94.

17. The best source on Schlesinger's background is Nick Thimmesch, "Professor in the Pentagon," *Washington Post/Potomac*, October 6, 1974, pp. 10-32.

18. U.S., Congress, Senate, Committee on Government Operations, *Memorandum, Planning-Programming-Budgeting, Uses and Abuses of Analysis*, 1968.

19. The best sources of Schlesinger's positions are his *Annual Defense Department Reports for FY 1975 and FY 1976*. The FY 1975 edition focuses primarily on the strategic area, while FY 1976 contains his arguments for a strong conventional force.

20. Enthoven and Smith, *How Much*, p. 175, and Robert McNamara, *FY 1969 Defense Department Report*, January 1968, p. 50.

21. The Soviets began deploying MIRV in mid-1975.

22. Although this argument was developed by Schlesinger, it was not made public until January 1977 in Donald Rumsfeld, *FY 1978 Defense Report*, p. 68.

23. McNamara, *FY 1969 Defense Report*, p. 57.

24. Rumsfeld, *FY 1978 Defense Report*, p. 78.

25. For analyses of Schlesinger's strategic arguments see: Herbert Scoville, "Flexible Madness," *Foreign Policy*, Spring 1974, pp. 164-77; Ted Greenwood and Michael Nacht, "The New Nuclear Debate: Sense or Nonsense," *Foreign Affairs*, July 1974, pp. 761-80; and Lawrence Korb, "The Issues and Costs of the New United States Nuclear Policy," *Naval War College Review*, November-December 1974, pp. 28-41.

26. The press conference is reprinted in *Washington Post*, July 4, 1974, p. A7.

27. Quoted in Richard Levine, "The Pentagon Loses a Talented Leader," *Wall Street Journal*, November 3, 1975, p. 3.

28. For example, see Michael Getler, "Ironies in the Schlesinger Dismissal," *Washington Post*, November 6, 1975, p. A24.

29. Levine, "Pentagon Loses Leader," p. 3. In his forthcoming memoir, *A*

Time to Heal, former President Ford describes Schlesinger as arrogant, disdainful of the presidency, and disastrous in his dealings with Congress.

30. Rowland Evans and Robert Novak, "Schlesinger's Intolerable Dissent," *Washington Post,* November 6, 1975, p. A27.

31. For example, see Bernard Gwertzman, "Behind Shift: Push for an Arms Pact," *New York Times,* November 4, 1975, pp. 4, 26.

32. Getler, "Ironies," p. A24.

33. Schlesinger's remarks are contained in a Pentagon news briefing of September 19, 1975, and in his appearance on "Face the Nation," September 21, 1975.

34. Quoted in Gwertzman, "Behind Shift," p. 26.

35. John Hall, "Ford Backs Kissinger in Feud with Schlesinger," *Baltimore News-American,* October 2, 1975, p. 2.

36. Quoted in James Naughton, "Ford Prods 'Can't Do' Congress Over Fiscal Proposals," *New York Times,* October 11, 1975, p. 14.

37. George Wilson, "Schlesinger Warns of Illusions," *Washington Post,* November 11, 1975, p. A8.

38. In a Gallup poll taken in December 1975, 63 percent of the American public felt that during 1976 Russia would increase its military power. This compared to 55 percent in 1974 and 38 percent in 1965. George Gallup, "Public Uncertain about Future Power of the U.S.," *Providence Journal,* January 18, 1976, p. A16.

39. Details of the proposed agreement are outlined in Murray Marder, "Nuclear Talks Must Succeed on Two Fronts," *Washington Post,* February 23, 1977, p. A1.

40. George Wilson, "Rumsfeld: No Firing Role," *Washington Post,* November 13, 1975, p. A1. See also Donald Rumsfeld, *Annual Defense Department Report, FY 1977,* January 26, 1976.

41. Interview with William Clements, April 28, 1978, Dallas, Texas.

42. Donald Rumsfeld, *FY 1978 Defense Report,* p. 8.

43. Ibid., p. 307.

CHAPTER 4

The Military
Chiefs

Introduction

The Joint Chiefs of Staff (JCS) is composed of five military officers: the Chief of Staff of the Army, the Chief of Naval Operations (CNO), the Commandant of the Marine Corps (CMC), the Chief of Staff of the Air Force, and a chairman who can be from any service. Until an amendment to the FY 1979 Defense Authorization Act was enacted, the Commandant of the Marine Corps was not a voting member of the JCS and was supposed to participate only in those discussions of the JCS which pertained to the Marine Corps. However, since the early 1960s the CMC has become a full member of the JCS and has participated without inhibition in all its matters. The new law merely legitimized this situation. All of the Chiefs except the Chairman have dual responsibilities. In their joint capacity they are the principal military advisers to the President and the Secretary of Defense. In addition, each service Chief is the military head of his own service, responsible to the service secretaries (Secretary of the Army, Navy, Air Force) for training, organization, and readiness of forces. Figure 5 depicts the organizational relationship of the JCS within the defense establishment in 1977.

Civil-Military Disagreements in the Policy Process

Since its creation in 1947, the JCS has been a consistent source of irritation to the men for whom it worked. Several of the civilian secretaries who headed the Pentagon prior to 1968 saw many of their efforts undone because of conflicts with their military advisers.[1] At one time or another, all of the post-World War II presidents have accused the JCS of failing to fulfill its responsibilities in the policy process.

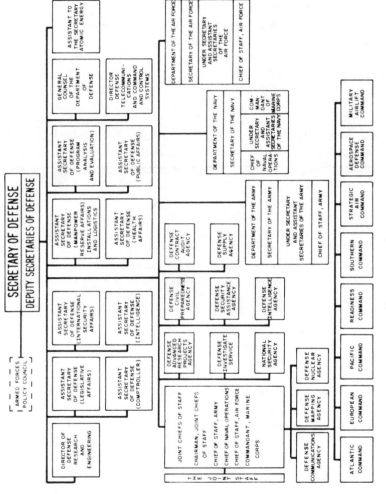

Figure 5 Department of Defense, 1977.

In the interim between the end of World War II and the outbreak of the Korean War, the JCS refused to advise Secretaries of Defense James Forrestal and Louis Johnson on how to create a balanced military force within the budget ceilings established by President Truman, or on how to divide the roles and missions among the military departments. Moreover, when the defense budget was finally presented to Congress by these secretaries, the JCS refused to take responsibility for it or endorse it. Partly as a result of their inability to work effectively with the Chiefs, both Forrestal and Johnson were fired by President Truman. The President himself was so upset at the actions of his Chiefs that he fired one, CNO Admiral Louis Denfeld, and put the "fear of God" into the others by threatening to cashier the rest if their behavior did not change. Only the outbreak of the Korean War, which necessitated a fivefold expansion in the size of our defense forces, put a temporary end to the disputes between the JCS and its civilian superiors in the Truman administration.

However, as soon as the Korean War came to a close, the Chiefs resumed their prewar behavior. During the 1953-1960 period, they refused to cooperate with Secretaries of Defense Charles Wilson and Neil McElroy either in developing long-range plans to support the Eisenhower policy of massive retaliation or in formulating a balanced force structure to conform to President Eisenhower's restrictive ceilings on the size of the defense budgets. The Secretaries had to develop their own long-range plans and make across-the-board or meat-ax reductions in the service budgets to bring them into line with the presidential ceilings. This inevitably resulted in poor plans and an unbalanced force posture. For example, during the 1950s, the Pentagon had twelve separate long-range missile programs but inadequate air and sealift forces.

The Chiefs added to the chaos in the Pentagon in the Eisenhower years by publicly condemning the national security policies of the President and his Secretary of State. Army Generals Maxwell Taylor and Matthew Ridgway accused the administration of trying to destroy the effectiveness of the Army, and of undermining this nation's ability to fight limited wars. Admiral Arleigh Burke complained that the Navy was still relying on World War II technology and weapon systems while Marine Generals Lemuel Shepherd and Randolph

Pate observed that the Marine Corps was short of men. Air Force Generals Nathan Twining and Thomas White warned Congress first about a bomber gap and then a missile gap.

As a former military officer, President Eisenhower was outraged at the behavior of the Chiefs. The more he exhorted them to be "team players," the more outspoken they became, especially in their congressional appearances. The Chief Executive responded by accusing the Chiefs of "legalized insubordination,"[2] forcing two of them to retire early, and trying to amend the National Security Act of 1947 so that the prerogative of the JCS to speak out against administration policy before the Congress would be taken away.

The conflicts between the JCS and their civilian superiors during the Truman and Eisenhower eras were mild compared to those that ensued between 1961 and 1968. Robert McNamara structured the decision process within DOD in such a way that for all practical purposes the Chiefs were excluded. In addition, the Secretary made a number of decisions which the Chiefs felt were militarily unsound. The first group of chiefs appointed by McNamara complained so vociferously about his methods and decisions that the strong-willed Secretary found it necessary to fire every single one of them. For fear of meeting the same fate as the first group, their successors initially did not criticize his methods or decisions. Indeed, they were so compliant that it seemed unnatural and unhealthy to many people.[3] However, when McNamara changed his mind about the utility of military force in Vietnam and thus began to lose some of his standing with Lyndon Johnson, the Chiefs seized this opening to go public with their disagreements with the Secretary. Moreover, they began to drop subtle hints that they were considering a mass resignation.[4] Their conduct placed so much pressure on President Johnson, who was having a difficult time keeping support for his Vietnam War policies, that he was forced to let McNamara go.

Neither President Kennedy nor President Johnson was very happy with the performance of the JCS. Kennedy was appalled that the JCS did not oppose more forcefully the militarily unsound landing at the Bay of Pigs. Johnson was dismayed by the lack of imagination and creativity that the Chiefs displayed in their advice about Vietnam. Johnson complained that throughout the course of the war all the Chiefs could recommend was "bomb, bomb, bomb."[5]

Interservice Rivalry

In addition to clashing with the Secretary of Defense, the pre-1969 members of the JCS often undermined the Pentagon's credibility by publicly condemning the programs of each other's services. Prior to the Korean War, the Army and the Air Force Chiefs were openly skeptical of the Navy's attempts to build aircraft carriers and the Marine Corps' desire to preserve an amphibious warfare capability. Naval leaders, for their part, criticized the capability of the Air Force's B-36 bomber to reach targets in the Soviet Union. In fact, public criticism of the entire B-36 program by Naval officers became so intense and irrational that Congress felt it necessary to conduct a lengthy investigation of the situation.[6]

During the 1950s such outspoken military Chiefs as Maxwell Taylor and Arleigh Burke openly feuded over the shares of the budget allotted to the other services.[7] In the early 1960s, leaders of the Air Force and the Navy opposed the Army's ABM program; the Air Force and Army Chiefs were critical of the Navy's attempts to build a nuclear-powered fleet; and the uniformed heads of the Army and Navy would not support a new manned bomber for the Air Force.

In the post-Vietnam period, recurrence of civil-military conflicts or another outbreak of interservice rivalry would have destroyed the efforts of the Secretaries of Defense to accomplish their goals. However, in the post-1969 period none of these situations occurred. In fact, during this time there was a complete turnabout in the conduct of the Chiefs. The JCS and the Secretaries of Defense appeared to complement each other. The Chiefs not only endorsed the programs of Laird, Schlesinger, and Rumsfeld, they actually helped the Secretaries to put their programs into effect. One example was their making the reductions in manpower and weapon systems that enabled Laird to meet Nixon's rigid budget ceilings. Similarly, the Chiefs cooperated with each other. Rather than seeking to undermine the prerogatives of the other services, the JCS looked for ways in which the services could complement each other. For example, the Air Force was given a role in sea control and the Marines a role in the defense of Europe. The conduct of the Chiefs confounded the experts who assumed that a period of tight budgets would inevitably lead to a period of civil-military hostility and interservice rivalry.[8]

The primary reason why the JCS had such excellent relationships with the Secretary and with each other was that their backgrounds were appropriate for the post-Vietnam period. The remainder of this chapter will compare their backgrounds to those of their predecessors and then analyze the most significant actions of these military professionals in dealing with the realities of the post-Vietnam period.[9] The list of men appointed to the JCS by Laird and Schlesinger is in Table 29.

Chairmen

Prior to the Nixon administration, the senior military position in this nation's armed forces, the chairmanship of the JCS, had been held almost exclusively by Army generals. In the twenty-year period between 1949, when the position was first established, and 1969, an Army officer had occupied the post for fifteen years, and four of the six appointees to the post were Army generals. In addition to the anxieties created by allowing one service to control the chairmanship for such a long period, the Army generals had also caused considerable discomfort among the other Chiefs due to their tendency to become involved in partisan politics. In March 1952, General Omar Bradley, the first Chairman, in a speech to the Pasadena Chamber of Commerce, publicly castigated the defense policies of Senator Robert Taft (R-Ohio), then the titular head of the Republican party and the front runner for the Republican presidential nomination. Taft was so upset at Bradley's speech that he made his support for Eisenhower contingent on the former general firing not just Bradley but the entire JCS.[10] The third Army officer to serve as Chairman, Maxwell Taylor, occupied a high-level political post in the White House under John Kennedy prior to returning to active duty to take the chairmanship. In addition, Taylor was a close personal friend of both the President and Robert Kennedy.[11] Therefore, the other Chiefs were not certain where his loyalties lay. During Taylor's tenure as Chairman, the service Chiefs were often hesitant to reveal their true feelings in JCS meetings for fear that they would be transmitted to the White House. General Earl Wheeler, the Army officer who succeeded Taylor as Chairman, was widely regarded as a Taylor protégé. Moreover, Wheeler also had White House connec-

Table 29 Members of the Joint Chiefs of Staff in the Post-Vietnam Period

Chairman	Army	Navy	Air Force	Marines
Thomas Moorer 7/70-7/74	Creighton Abrams 9/72-9/74	Elmo Zumwalt 7/70-7/74	John Ryan 8/69-8/73	Robert Cushman 1/72-6/75
George Brown 7/74-7/78	Frederick Weyand 9/74-9/76	James Holloway 7/74-7/78	George Brown 9/73-7/74	Louis Wilson 7/75-6/79
			David Jones 7/74-7/78	

Laird 1/69-1/73
Schlesinger 5/73-11/75

tions, having briefed John Kennedy during the 1960 presidential campaign.

In the post-1969 period, the military could not afford any connection with partisan politics. Its stock had already declined severely because of the moral ambiguities of the Vietnam War. Nor did the Pentagon need internal dissension among the services. The fiscal and political realities made it imperative that the services appreciate each other's functions and not revive the interservice rivalries that had followed World War II and Korea.

These conditions made it necessary for the position of Chairman to be held by officers with broad-based military backgrounds who appreciated the contributions of and were respected by the other services and were free from any connection with partisanship. It was also desirable that the post of Chairman go to officers of the Navy and the Air Force. Interservice harmony required that these two services be allocated some time at the top of the military hierarchy, and since the Army had been identified so closely with the war in Vietnam, it would have been difficult for an Army general to preside over Vietnamization.

The officers appointed to the chairmanship by Laird and Schlesinger met these criteria quite well. Laird selected Admiral Thomas Moorer, who served from 1970 to 1974, while Schlesinger chose Air Force General George Brown, who served for the next four years. In addition to giving the other services representation, both Moorer and Brown were professionals who brought excellent backgrounds to the JCS and were held in high esteem by their colleagues from the other services. Each had graduated from a senior service college and each had served on the JCS as the head of his own service. Moorer was the first naval officer to have commanded both the Atlantic and Pacific fleets, and Brown was the first Air Force officer to have had command experience in strategic, tactical, and logistic aircraft as well as a technical area. Finally, both Moorer and Brown had significant experience outside their own services. Moorer participated in the Strategic Bombing Survey after World War II, while Brown was the Military Assistant to Secretaries of Defense Gates and McNamara and to General Earl Wheeler while the latter was serving as Chairman of the JCS. Moreover, neither Moorer nor Brown owed his rise to the top of the military profession to any outside political influence.

Compared to the backgrounds of the other naval and Air Force officers who had been chairmen, Moorer and Brown were especially experienced. The first naval officer to serve as Chairman (1953-1957), Arthur Radford, was a thorough-going Navy partisan who had fought against unification of the military establishment in the post-World War II period and had led the "Revolt of the Admirals" in 1949 when the Secretary of Defense refused to allow the Navy to have a significant role in strategic bombing.[12] He was appointed Chairman without having served on the JCS as the Chief of Naval Operations (CNO). Radford's tenure in office was marked by acrimony and bitterness among the Chiefs and between the JCS and the administration. Because he had not served as a service Chief, Radford was unfamiliar with the organizational norms of the JCS. Consequently, he did not realize that the Chairman is a first among equals, who leads by persuasion rather than by fiat. He attempted to manage the JCS as he did his carrier task force. Radford "ordered" the JCS to support the Eisenhower defense policy and when they would not, he openly criticized his colleagues and excluded them from many steps in the decision-making process. One of the service Chiefs compared Radford to a party whip.[13]

The fact that Radford had not been the Chief of Naval Operations prior to becoming Chairman also brought him into conflict with the men who were CNOs during his tenure. Radford tried to dictate policy for the Navy as well as the JCS despite the fact that he had no responsibilities for the service and that Admirals Arleigh Burke and Robert Carney insisted that he keep out of naval affairs. Radford eventually became so frustrated with the difficulties of getting along with his fellow officers that he refused Eisenhower's offer of reappointment and retired.

The only other Air Force officer to serve as Chairman prior to 1974 was General Nathan Twining (1957-1960). Twining was primarily a product of the strategic bombing command. He did not attend a senior service college and lacked any significant joint experience. Consequently, Twining saw strategic air power as the primary solution to this nation's defense problems. This attitude caused him difficulties with the other Chiefs and the administration that were similar to those experienced by Radford, and Twining resigned for health reasons before completing a normal tour as Chairman.

Moorer's four years in office were among the most difficult faced by any Chairman. The naval officer was placed in a number of difficult situations which, if mishandled, could have had disastrous consequences for DOD, the military profession, and the nation. Yet Moorer handled each of these situations so adroitly that he kept the confidence of both his civilian superiors in the executive and legislative branches and his colleagues on the JCS. These situations may be placed into two categories.

First, he had to convince his colleagues on the JCS not only to accommodate themselves to the reduced levels of defense spending that characterized the 1969-1975 period and the withdrawal from Vietnam, but to support those policies before Congress. To prevent internal disagreements among the Chiefs over how to split the reduced defense budget and how rapidly United States forces should be withdrawn from Vietnam from becoming public, Moorer often had to "throw oil upon troubled waters" and convince the Chiefs to withdraw their formal dissenting positions.[14] For example, in December 1970, Admiral Elmo Zumwalt, the Chief of Naval Operations, argued that the budget reductions which the Nixon administration had mandated for FY 1972 impacted most severely upon the Navy. As a consequence, Zumwalt stated that the Navy had only a 50-percent chance of defeating the rapidly growing Soviet Navy. When Zumwalt wanted to add a footnote to this effect to a JCS paper titled "Worldwide Posture of U.S. Military Forces," Army Chief of Staff William Westmoreland, Marine Corps Commandant General Leonard Chapman, and Air Force Chief of Staff General John Ryan all objected. Each of these service Chiefs argued that, comparatively speaking, the Navy was better off than his own service. Therefore, if the Navy added a footnote, there should be one for each other service as well. Chairman Moorer defused the situation by proposing that if Zumwalt would withdraw his footnote, Moorer's own staff, the Joint Staff, would do a detailed study on the specific capabilities of each service.[15]

Similarly, in 1971, Moorer was responsible for getting the Army Chief of Staff to support an agreement between General Creighton Abrams, then Commander of U.S. Forces in Vietnam, and the Commandant of the Marine Corps that the Marines would withdraw first from Vietnam. The Army Chief initially resisted the arrangement because of the additional cost that would accrue to his service from remaining in Vietnam.[16] So successful was Moorer in holding the JCS together that from 1972 through 1974 only three memorandums of non-concurrence were submitted, two by the Army and one by the Air Force.

Moorer also persuaded his colleagues not to be overly pessimistic about the deterioration in the military balance caused by the Soviets' increasing their defense effort while ours was being cut back. Moorer had three reasons for urging this course of action. First, public complaints about the level of defense spending by an individual service Chief could easily degenerate into criticism of another service. This was precisely what happened in the period between the end of World War II and the outbreak of the Korean War; each service Chief argued that postwar demobilization should fall most heavily on the other services. Second, pessimistic evaluations, rather than encouraging Congress to do more, could lead the legislative branch to feel "what's the use" and do less. Third, some members of Congress would use the views of the Chiefs to embarrass the administration. In the immediate post-Vietnam period, Congress was much less sympathetic to defense than the administration and there is little doubt that public dissent by the Chiefs would have boomeranged.[17]

A second delicate situation which Moorer had to face was that he was often caught between the Secretary of Defense and the White House. As Chairman of the JCS, Moorer had responsibilities to both. Theoretically, the President and the Secretary of Defense should have been working in tandem. However, neither Nixon nor Kissinger was very fond of Laird or of a number of his positions. For example, the Secretary of Defense opposed the decision to invade Cambodia in April 1970 and Laos in February 1971.[18] As was noted in the previous chapter, Laird had not been Nixon's original choice for the post. However, because of Laird's wide support with Congress and the Republican party, neither the President nor his assistant wanted to confront him directly. When someone leaked the fact that Laird and Secretary of State Rogers opposed the Cambodian invasion, Nixon only called Rogers and told him to get behind the decision.[19] Therefore, both the President and his Assistant for National Security Affairs often dealt directly with the Chairman. For example, during the bombing of Hanoi in December of 1972 and the Indo-Pakistan War of December of 1971, the White House bypassed

Laird and communicated directly with Moorer. Moreover, on a number of other occasions Moorer was given information by the White House with specific orders not to share it with Laird. Moorer handled these situations by never taking action without first clearing it with Laird.[20] So adroitly did Moorer do this that throughout his tenure in office he was able to keep the confidence of Nixon, Laird, and Kissinger.

During his four years as Chairman, General George Brown became best known for a series of three indiscreet and intemperate sets of remarks about some very sensitive subjects. At a Duke Law School Forum in October 1974, Brown complained about Israel's undue influence on Congress but inaccurately ascribed that influence to the fact that the Jewish people in this country own the banks and newspapers. Two years later, Brown stated that from a military point of view, the American commitment to Israel was a burden on the United States. Finally, in March 1977, the Chairman vigorously defended the right of the government to spy on American citizens in order to protect national security. Normally, remarks similar to those made by General Brown would have resulted in immediate dismissal by the President or irreparable harm to the military profession. However, the fact that neither occurred says something about Brown's capabilities and the "rise of the Pentagon."

Brown was not relieved by the President simply because he was too valuable as Chairman of the JCS. Indeed, former President Ford paid a heavy political price for keeping Brown as Chairman. The Air Force general's initial remarks were most offensive to the Jews, who are a key voting bloc in the many populous states which Ford needed to win in the 1976 election. It was particularly difficult for Ford to keep Brown in office when his next remarks were made public during the 1976 presidential campaign.

Brown's value as Chairman came from three sources. First, he was a superb military strategist with great expertise on the complex issues involved in the SALT negotiations. President Carter, who had once called for Brown's dismissal, described him as "the outstanding military leader and strategist that we have in America today."[21] Brown's capabilities in this area of strategic weaponry were unmatched by any of the other Chiefs. Moreover, SALT was the primary issue during Brown's tenure as Chairman. Second, Brown held a balanced analytical view of the military situation between the

United States and the USSR. Unlike some of his contemporaries, he was neither inclined to overstate the Soviet military threat nor understate America's military capabilities. In his annual reports to Congress, his congressional testimony, and his public speeches Brown effectively refuted the arguments of extremists on both sides.[22] Third, Brown was held in high regard by his military colleagues for his honesty and expertise. For example, during 1975, his first full year in office, not one of the other Chiefs forwarded a memorandum of non-concurrence to a JCS decision. Brown was frank and outspoken with both his subordinates and superiors. His advice on military affairs was never dulled in transmission. The Air Force general never tried to anticipate the consensus or give the advice the senior officials wanted to hear. Moreover, from a military point of view, Brown's advice was always sound. Indeed, if the truth be known, most military officers share Brown's opinion that Israel is a military burden on the United States and resent the impact of Israel on our national security policy over the past twenty-five years. As one of Brown's contemporaries on the JCS noted:

America's commitment to Israel involves a formidable array of military risks. It drains arms the services badly need to keep themselves in a state of readiness. It jeopardizes sources of oil we and our allies depend upon. It puts us on what might turn out to be a collision course with the USSR in a part of the world where they have almost all the advantages. It strains our relations with our NATO allies.[23]

The fact that Brown's intemperate remarks, made during the period from 1974 through early 1977, did not harm the military profession was a measure of how far the military had recovered from its Vietnam decline. During that time its standing with the public rose; in fact, the military became the most admired profession.[24] Even Brown's severest detractors considered him an "anachronism, hardly typical of the well prepared, broad gauged, politically aware younger officers increasingly available for leadership responsibilities in the post-Vietnam armed forces."[25]

The Army

When Laird became Secretary of Defense, General William Westmoreland was serving as Army Chief of Staff. He had been placed in that position by Lyndon Johnson shortly after the Tet offensive in order to remove him tactfully from Vietnam where his battlefield tactics had proved disastrous. If anything, Westmoreland was worse in Washington than he had been in Saigon. He did not seem capable of coping with the changing environment that confronted the military in the post-Vietnam period. During his tenure as Chief of Staff, he was preoccupied primarily with justifying his role in Vietnam.[26] His Army subordinates became disenchanted and even embarrassed with his performance in the Pentagon. For example, during the Jordanian civil war of September 1970, Westmoreland made the somewhat innane proposal of sending an Army brigade to Cyprus, or Turkey, or Greece.[27] In the Army section within the Pentagon, the acronym GROW appeared in many places. It stood for "Get Rid of Westmoreland." As the end of Westmoreland's tenure neared, GROW became GROWN, "Get Rid of Westmoreland Now!"

When Westmoreland's term expired in the summer of 1972, Laird selected General Creighton Abrams to succeed him. Many considered Abrams, at fifty-eight, too old to take on the job of leading the Army in the post-Vietnam period; Laird, however, was convinced that Abrams was the man to help the Army adapt to the new environment. The Secretary had observed firsthand how well Abrams had adapted traditional Army strategy to the jungles of Vietnam and how successfully he had managed the massive American withdrawal from Southeast Asia, along with the Vietnamization that made possible the Paris Peace Accords of 1973. In addition, Laird remembered Abram's excellent handling of a potentially explosive situation when he served as the Commanding Officer of the Army troops sent to Mississippi in 1962 to enforce the admission of James Meredith to the University of Mississippi.[28] Abrams did not disappoint Laird or Schlesinger. He quickly shifted the focus of the Army from Vietnam toward the future. He reorganized the Army's command structure, improved its combat-to-support ratio, and laid the foundation for an increase of three combat divisions without an increase in manpower. Unfortunately, after only two years in the Army's top position, Abrams died of lung cancer.

In the fall of 1974, Schlesinger ensured that Abrams's initiatives and leadership style would be continued by selecting General Frederick Weyand to succeed him. Although Weyand was not a graduate of West Point and was not well known in Army circles, he had been

Abrams's principal deputy in both Vietnam and the Pentagon, and in that capacity had helped the late general formulate his policies in both places. Moreover, unlike most of his predecessors, Weyand had had broad experience in both the staff and line branches of the Army. For the first nine years of his military career, Weyand was in the intelligence branch. During the Korean War, he switched to combat arms and commanded a battalion in Korea and a division and field force in Vietnam.

In his two years in office, Weyand successfully implemented Abrams's program of reducing the Army's support forces and increasing its combat capabilities. When he retired voluntarily in the fall of 1976, Weyand left the Army with sixteen divisions, a procurement budget more than two times higher than when he took over, and some ten thousand less support and ten thousand more combat troops.

In addition, Weyand performed an extremely valuable function for the nation. In April 1975, he traveled to South Vietnam and correctly determined that the Thieu government would soon collapse. This realistic appraisal of the situation by a man who had spent so many years in Vietnam and had been the last U.S. Commander there prepared the American public for the rapid and unexpected fall of Saigon later that month. Weyand's candid assessment was in sharp contrast to the unduly optimistic reports of military officers sent to analyze the Vietnam situation in previous years.[29]

Navy

The Navy is one of the most entrenched bureaucracies in the federal government. Traditionally, it has resisted all forms of change. In the post-World War II period, the Navy successively fought against the integration of blacks within its ranks; it opposed the efforts of the other services and the Truman administration to unify the military into one department; and it resisted efforts to place the strategic missiles on its Polaris and Poseidon submarines under a joint target-planning group. The Navy's cooperation in joint ventures with the other services and defense agencies usually is grudging and normally minimal. Laird recognized that in order to force the naval bureaucracy to adjust to the new environment, the sea service would need a new type of leader. Accordingly, in 1970, he selected Vice Admiral Elmo Zumwalt over thirty-seven more senior admirals to become the nineteenth Chief of Naval Operations. At forty-nine, Zumwalt was the youngest man to take over the Navy and a full five years younger than the mean age of the eighteen previous CNOs. Unlike most of his predecessors, who made their mark in seagoing commands, Zumwalt had spent considerable time in the Pentagon. He had been senior aide to the Secretary of the Navy, head of the Navy's Systems Analysis Division, and head of the Arms Control Division in the Office of the Assistant Secretary of Defense for International Security Affairs. Therefore, Zumwalt was quite familiar with the workings of the national security bureaucracy and was quite skilled in the art of bureaucratic politics.

Despite his youth and comparative lack of operational experience, Zumwalt shook the foundations of the Navy to its core during his four years in office. Using messages dubbed "Z Grams," Zumwalt issued 120 directives which liberalized personnel policies, improved the living conditions of enlisted men, abolished petty chicken regulations, and made the Navy more appealing to minorities. Although his directives caused a great deal of controversy within the Navy, the changes in personnel policies were quite effective. During his tenure, desertion and unauthorized absence rates reached all-time lows. In a non-draft environment, Navy reenlistment rates rose from 12 to 38 percent for first-term enlistees and from 80 to 91 percent for career personnel. The number of black enlisted men and the number of blacks in the officer corps nearly doubled during the Zumwalt years.[30]

While many members of the naval hierarchy were outraged by Zumwalt's personnel policies, he kept their support with his successes in the hardware area. With prodding from Schlesinger, then at the Bureau of the Budget, Zumwalt reduced maintenance costs by scrapping four hundred of the Navy's older ships. He then shifted the funds into the procurement of newer, more modern ships. During his tenure, the Navy received more investment funds than the Army and Air Force combined, and the Navy's share of the DOD budget climbed from 27.2 percent to 32.2 percent. Moreover, through Zumwalt's intensive lobbying efforts on Capitol Hill and throughout the country, the Navy's budgets were treated more kindly than those of the other services by Congress.

As Zumwalt's four-year term neared completion, there was a great deal of uneasiness within the Navy about his successor. The traditionalists felt that the Navy could not endure four more years of turmoil. The service needed a "thermidor period," that is, time to digest the 450 changes enacted by Zumwalt. The modernizers feared that any attempt to turn back the clock would drive down reenlistment rates. Zumwalt's supporters argued that the post-Vietnam era could not tolerate a nineteenth-century Navy. Schlesinger satisfied both groups when he chose Admiral James Holloway III to succeed Zumwalt. The traditionalists were pleased because Holloway came from an old Navy family. Both his father and father-in-law were admirals. The modernizers could not complain because Zumwalt had chosen Holloway to be his Vice Chief of Naval Operations. Zumwalt pronounced himself perfectly satisfied with the choice of Holloway as his successor.[31]

In addition to bridging the gap between the traditionalists and the modernizers, Holloway had several other qualifications for the Navy's top post. He was the first CNO to be associated with all of the Navy's major line officer factions or unions. In World War II, Holloway served on surface ships in both the Atlantic and Pacific theaters. As a gunnery officer on board the destroyer *Bennion*, the CNO took part in the largest naval surface battle in history—the Battle of Surigao Straits. During the Korean War, the Lebanon landing, and the Quemoy-Matsu crisis, he was a combat pilot. In the mid-1960s, he graduated from the nuclear power school conducted by Admiral Hyman Rickover, the Navy's most distinguished submariner. Finally, Holloway had commanded both nuclear-powered and conventional ships.

During his four years in office, Holloway pleased both groups and justified Schlesinger's expectations by his middle-of-the-road policy. He did not undertake any wholesale revision of Zumwalt's policies nor did he initiate very many new dramatic changes. In the area of personnel, he provided the Navy with the "thermidor period" it so badly needed.

Holloway also performed well in other areas. In hardware, Holloway succeeded in reversing the downward trend in the numbers of ships. Because of his procurement policies the size of the Navy will increase from its 1979 level of 438 ships to almost 500 by the mid-1980s. The CNO also provided a needed sense of perspective to the discussion about the capabilities of the Soviet Navy vis-à-vis our own. Holloway did not join forces with those "prophets of doom" who claimed that the Soviet Union is vastly superior to the United States in naval power and that the U.S. Navy can no longer carry out its responsibilities. Rather, he argued that the Soviet Navy is clearly superior to the U.S. Navy only in the area of attack submarines. In Holloway's view, the two navies are about even in cruisers, destroyers, frigates, and amphibious ships while this nation is vastly superior in air power at sea because of its carrier force. Throughout his tenure he assured the nation that the Navy could carry out its responsibilities within the national strategy in any likely confrontation.[32] Finally, Holloway laid the foundation for the next technological breakthrough in naval warfare, vertical take-off and landing aircraft. When these planes are introduced, every naval platform will acquire offensive air capability and the striking power of the fleet will increase by a large order of magnitude.[33]

The Air Force

From its creation as a separate service in 1947 through the Vietnam era, the Air Force was headed by seven men who made their reputations with the Strategic Air Command (SAC). These men had flown manned bombers in World War II and during the Cold War they had developed a fleet of long-range bombers which for over a decade provided our primary strategic deterrent. To these Air Force Chiefs, the manned penetrating bombers were the essence of the Air Force, and they forcefully resisted even the most persuasive arguments against the continued utility of these planes in the missile era. For example, in 1962, Curtis LeMay, the Air Force Chief of Staff, admitted to Congress that he could not refute the arguments that Secretary McNamara had proposed against LeMay's plan to build a follow-up to the B-52 bomber. Yet, he urged Congress to appropriate funds for a newer bomber, the B-70.[34]

The fixation of these men with long-range manned bombers was not difficult to understand. They did not attend any civilian or military postgraduate schools and had almost no association with the other branches of their own service. For example, John Ryan, the Chief of Staff in the first years of the Nixon administration, had spent only two years of his entire career outside of SAC. He was Inspector General for one year and Vice Chief of Staff for another.

Unfortunately for the Air Force and its leaders, the golden age of the manned bomber ended very quickly. By the early 1960s, the strategic deterrent of this nation had shifted to land- and sea-based missiles, particularly the latter. Fortunately for the Air Force, Schlesinger's choices to succeed Ryan did not have exclusive SAC backgrounds. Although both George Brown and David Jones have had tours with SAC, each man had wide experience in tactical and logistic aircraft operations and had a wide variety of staff and operational assignments. Under their leadership, the Air Force moved away from its nearly exclusive orientation toward the manned bomber and began to give equal emphasis to its tactical and airlift components and to developing weapons such as the cruise missile, which could eliminate the need for penetrating bombers. As a result of the efforts of Brown and Jones, the Tactical Air Force grew from 1,400 aircraft in 1970 to 1,650 in 1976 and will grow to 2,500 by 1980. Despite fiscal constraints, Brown and Jones succeeded in more than doubling the annual procurement rates for these planes. These men were also responsible for the Air Force's willingness to take control of all military airlift for DOD. Finally, when President Carter decided not to build the B-1 bomber, the Air Force, rather than wasting its energies trying to overturn the decision, enthusiastically embarked on full-scale development of the air-launched cruise missile.

The Marine Corps

The right of the Commandant of the Marine Corps to participate in JCS matters of direct concern to this service was first sanctioned by the passage of the Mansfield-Douglas Act in 1952. Prior to that time, the Commandant not only was excluded from all JCS deliberations but the very existence of the Marine Corps as a separate service was in doubt. Indeed, Secretary of Defense George Marshall, CNO Admiral Forrest Sherman, and Army Chief of Staff General Lawton Collins opposed the Mansfield-Douglas Act, which in addition to giving the Commandant conditional representation on the JCS, legislatively guaranteed the separate existence of the Marine Corps by fixing its peacetime strength at three divisions and three air wings.

Initially, the Commandants interpreted the phrase "JCS matters of direct concern to the Marine Corps" very narrowly. In 1952, General Lemuel Shepherd exercised his right to join in JCS deliberations in only 8 percent of the issues that came before the Chiefs.[35] By the end of the decade, the Commandant still participated in less than half of the matters which were discussed by the JCS. For example, General Randolph Pate, who served as Commandant through 1960, participated in only 37 percent of the deliberations of the JCS.

The Commandant of the Marine Corps evolved into an equal member of the JCS during the 1960s. During the 1960-1963 period, when David Shoup served as Commandant, participation of the Marine Corps in JCS matters crossed the 50 percent threshold for the first time. Shoup's successor, General Wallace Greene, became involved so extensively in JCS matters that in 1967, his last year in office, the Marine Corps was involved in 94.5 percent of the issues which came before the JCS.

However, the full participation of Shoup and Greene in JCS matters did not contribute very much to interservice harmony. Shoup dismayed his fellow Chiefs by alternating between the roles of skeptic, gadfly, devil's advocate, and dove. He broke with the service Chiefs on such important matters as the Laotian crisis of 1961 and the nuclear test-ban treaty of 1963. Although Shoup was well liked by President Kennedy, his military colleagues isolated him professionally and Shoup considered himself a failure as a member of the JCS.[36]

Greene, on the other hand, created problems with his fellow Chiefs because of his extreme hawkishness on the issue of sending ground troops to Vietnam. His bellicosity particularly annoyed the Army because the Marines' assault mission did not entail the follow-up mission of the Army to occupy territory.[37] Greene also irritated some of the other Chiefs by refusing to allow Marine Corps aircraft in Vietnam to be used to support Army troops despite the fact that this step was endorsed by General Westmoreland and Admiral Ulysses S. Grant Sharp, the Commander in Chief of the Pacific.[38]

The men who have been appointed as Commandant in the post-Vietnam period have not experienced the same problems as Shoup and Greene. Robert Cushman, who was selected by Laird in late

1971, and General Louis Wilson, appointed by Schlesinger in July 1975, have continued to participate in well over 95 percent of JCS matters. Yet neither of these men ever submitted a memorandum of non-concurrence on a JCS matter. Moreover, both have broadened the role of the Marine Corps in our national strategy. They have agreed to help offset the shortfall in Navy carrier-based aircraft by providing Marine aircraft and have transformed some elements of the Marine Corps so that they are capable of taking part in the defense of northern and central Europe.

A Composite View

In addition to possessing unique qualifications for heading their own services, the military officers appointed to the JCS by Laird and Schlesinger shared certain common characteristics which helped them prevent the problems of the pre-1968 period and cope with the post-1968 environment. These characteristics fall into five categories: regional origins, source of commission, advanced education, limited war experience, and prior involvement in the national security decision-making process.

Regional Origins

For the most part, during the height of the war in Vietnam, the JCS was dominated by southerners. The men who ran the Navy from 1963 through 1970, Admirals David McDonald and Thomas Moorer, were from Georgia and Alabama, respectively. John McConnell, the Air Force Chief of Staff from 1965 to 1969, was reared in Arkansas, while his Army counterpart, William Westmoreland, hailed from South Carolina.

In contrast, the men appointed by Laird and Schlesinger represented all of the geographic regions of the country. Admiral Zumwalt and General Weyand were from the Far West. Generals Abrams and Brown orginally came from the Northeast, while Generals Ryan, Cushman, and Jones were midwesterners. Admiral Moorer, whom Laird moved from CNO to Chairman, and General Wilson, whom Schlesinger named as Commandant in mid-1975, were the only southerners on the JCS during the post-Vietnam period. Admiral

Holloway entered the Naval Academy from Texas, but since his father was a career naval officer, Holloway cannot be classified as a southerner.

While it is difficult to make a direct connection between the regional origins of the Chiefs and their subsequent behavior, this concentration of men from the South was not a healthy situation, especially during a war which received more support in the South than in other sections of the nation. In addition, a military hierarchy dominated by southerners could have posed image problems for an organization trying to attract a representative and broad-based all-volunteer military force. It may have reinforced the stereotype of the military as a conservative institution run by white southern gentlemen.

Sources of Commission

The commissions of military officers come primarily from three sources: the service academies, the reserve officer training corps (ROTC), and officer candidate school (OCS). In the 1947-1969 period, approximately 95 percent of the Chiefs were graduates of the service academies.[39] However, this has not been the case in the post-Vietnam period. Under Laird and Schlesinger, membership in the JCS was broadened to include officers from ROTC and OCS. For example, General Weyand, who headed the Army from 1974 to 1976, is a product of the ROTC unit at the University of California at Berkeley, while General Jones, Air Force Chief of Staff from 1974 to 1978 and the present Chairman of the JCS, received his commission from OCS. Thus, during the 1974-1976 period, only half of the service Chiefs were products of military academies.

Widening the base from which the Chiefs were recruited had two beneficial effects. First, it brought men with broader backgrounds to the top of the military hierarchy. Prior to 1969, the service academies had a single-track technical curriculum, almost devoid of sociohumanistic electives. They were training schools rather than colleges. Thus, they tended to produce individuals with a narrow, rigid outlook.[40] Second, it increased morale among the non-academy graduates in the officer corps. These individuals received the message that opportunities would no longer be foreclosed simply because of the source of one's commission.

Advanced Education

Prior to 1969, thirty men were appointed to the JCS by the first nine secretaries of defense. Only fourteen were graduates of one of the five senior service colleges operated by the Pentagon. When one takes into account that these colleges were created specifically to prepare colonels and Navy captains to transcend their technical warfighting specialties and take on the broad responsibilities of general officers, it is astonishing that less than half of the men appointed to the JCS between 1947 and 1969 to operate the entire military establishment did not attend any of the senior service colleges. Moreover, only seven of these first thirty appointees attended the National War College. That institution's specific mission is to provide officers with the background and skills to function effectively in high-level joint assignments. With this lack of education, it is not hard to understand the difficulties that many of the pre-1969 Chiefs had in coping with the demands of their office.

Every one of the ten men selected to serve on the JCS by Laird and Schlesinger attended a senior service college and seven of these eight officers were graduates of the National War College. In fact, by mid-1975 all of the members of the JCS were alumni of the National War College. This was the first time that the entire membership of the JCS had attended that school.

Limited War Experience

Only one of the members of the JCS who made the critical inputs about the way the United States should conduct the war in Vietnam had any experience with limited war. Harold Johnson, Army Chief of Staff from 1964 to 1968, was in Korea from mid-1950 to mid-1951. His contemporaries on the JCS in the 1964-1968 period, that is, from the Gulf of Tonkin incident to the bombing halt, had not seen action in Korea. Admirals McDonald and Moorer and Generals Wheeler, LeMay, Greene, and McConnell had no actual warfighting experience outside of the total war environment of World War II.

In contrast, the appointees of Laird and Schlesinger had extensive combat experience in both Korea and Vietnam. During the Korean War, Admiral Elmo Zumwalt served as navigator on board the battleship *Wisconsin* which was involved in shelling coastal fortifications in both North and South Korea. For the two years prior to his selection as CNO, Zumwalt commanded all of the naval forces in Vietnam. His successor, James Holloway, flew jet fighters from aircraft carriers deployed off the Korean coast during the hostilities on that peninsula, while during the early days of the war in Vietnam he made two combat deployments to the Gulf of Tonkin as commander of the nuclear-powered carrier *Enterprise*. In the war's later stages, Holloway commanded the Seventh Fleet, which conducted the Navy's portion of the air war against Vietnam.

The situation was the same for the other services. General Creighton Abrams was Chief of Staff for three different Army corps assigned to the Korea theater and, in the five years immediately preceding his appointment as Army Chief of Staff, Abrams served successively as Deputy Commander and Commander of the Military Assistance Command (MACV) in Vietnam. His successor, General Frederick Weyand, was an infantry battalion commander in Korea, while in Vietnam he commanded successively a division, a field force, and, eventually, the entire MACV. During the last year of the Korean War, General George Brown was the Director of Operations for the Fifth Air Force, while for two years during the war in Vietnam he held the highest Air Force job in Southeast Asia, that is, command of the Seventh Air Force and Deputy for Air Operations to General Abrams at MACV. His successor as Air Force Chief of Staff, General David Jones, flew three hundred hours in combat missions over North Korea as a member of the Nineteenth Bombardment Squadron. In Vietnam, Jones served with Brown as the Vice Commander of the Seventh Air Force. General Cushman was not involved in the Korean War but during the war in Vietnam he commanded the III Marine Amphibious Force, assigned to the Southeast Asian area. This was the largest combat unit ever commanded by a Marine officer. General Wilson served with Marine divisions in both Korea and Vietnam.

This experience in all types of war defused one potential source of conflict between the Secretary of Defense and the JCS. During the *Mayaguez* incident, the JCS supported Schlesinger's position that the United States apply only limited force to free the captive merchant crew. (Secretary of State Kissinger's position was for the United States to attack Cambodia with B-52s.) During the war in Vietnam, the JCS and Secretary of Defense McNamara were constantly at loggerheads over the amount of force to apply in Southeast

Asia. The Chiefs, with their World War II backgrounds, consistently urged the policy makers to expand the scope and intensity of our involvement while McNamara sought to restrict the air and ground war in Southeast Asia.

Involvement in the National Security Decision-making Process

One of the reasons that the pre-1969 Chiefs had great difficulty operating in the Washington environment was that many of them had not spent much time at the higher levels of the decision-making process prior to their selection to the JCS. For example, neither Admiral Anderson, CNO from 1961 to 1963, nor General Westmoreland, Army Chief from 1968 to 1972, had served in Washington as a flag officer. General John Ryan, Air Force Chief from 1969 to 1973, had spent only one year in Washington in his entire career! Such prior experience is often the only way for a military officer to understand how to play a meaningful role in the national security decision-making process.

All of the officers selected by Laird and Schlesinger had been deeply involved in the policy process prior to their appointments. General Abrams had seven years of experience on the Army Staff including three years as Vice Chief of Staff in the early days of Vietnam, while General Weyand served as a military assistant to two secretaries of the Army, the military adviser to the American delegation to the Paris Peace Conference, and the Vice Chief of Staff of the Army. After reaching the rank of Commander (O-5), Admiral Zumwalt spent more than half of his remaining career in Washington. He served as an aide to the Secretary of the Navy, worked in the office of the Assistant Secretary of Defense for International Security Affairs, and was the first director of the Navy's Systems Analysis Division. His successor as CNO, Admiral Holloway, was the first Vice Chief of Naval Operations ever to move up to the Navy's top position. General Brown spent ten years in the Washington arena. He served for four years as the Military Assistant to Secretaries of Defense Thomas Gates and Robert McNamara, for three years as the principal assistant to Chairman of the JCS Earl Wheeler, and for three years as head of the Air Force Systems Command. His successor as Air Force Chief of Staff, General David Jones, spent some five years on the Air Staff and served for two years as aide to Curtis LeMay. General

Cushman spent eleven years serving in high-level staff positions. He was Assistant for National Security Affairs for four years to Vice President Nixon and Deputy Director of the CIA for almost two years. In addition, Cushman held two major staff positions at Marine Corps Headquarters. His successor as Commandant, General Louis Wilson, spent eighteen months in the key post of Marine Corps liaison to Congress.

Conclusion

The men appointed to the JCS by Laird and Schlesinger helped these secretaries cope with the demands of the post-Vietnam era. Their ability to cooperate with their civilian superiors and with each other was in part a function of their unique backgrounds. However, the high quality of civilian and military leadership in the post-Vietnam period was not the only factor responsible for the resurgence of the Pentagon. External events also played a part.

Notes

1. The data for this section is drawn from my book, *The Joint Chiefs of Staff: The First Twenty-five Years* (Bloomington: Indiana University Press, 1976). See also, Richard Betts, *Soldiers, Statesmen and Cold War Crises* (Cambridge, Mass.: Harvard University Press, 1977), pp. 52-74.

2. Dwight Eisenhower, *Waging Peace* (Garden City, N.Y.: Doubleday, 1956), p. 356.

3. See, for example, the complaints of members of the House Armed Services Committee during hearings on the FY 1966 defense budget (House Committee on Armed Services, *Hearings on the FY 1966 Defense Budget,* p. 1331).

4. Townsend Hoopes, *The Limits of Intervention* (New York: McKay, 1969), pp. 139-224.

5. David Halbestram, *The Best and the Brightest* (New York: Random House, 1972), p. 564.

6. For a complete description of this episode see Paul Hammond, "Super-carriers and B-36 Bombers," in *American Civil-Military Decisions* (Tuscaloosa: University of Alabama Press, 1963), pp. 467-553.

7. Maxwell Taylor, *The Uncertain Trumpet* (New York: Harper, 1960), discusses this era.

8. See, for example, Clark Murdock, *Defense Policy Formulation* (Albany: State University of New York Press, 1976), p. 174.

9. Background data comes from the official biographies supplied by the Public Affairs offices of the respective services. See also, *Current Biography* and *Who's Who in America.*

10. Samuel Huntington, *The Soldier and the State* (New York: Vintage, 1957), p. 386. See also, Lawrence Korb, "The Joint Chiefs of Staff in 1975: New Men for a New Reality," paper delivered at the 1975 Conference of the Inter-University Seminar on the Armed Forces and Society, Chicago, pp. 1-2.

11. One of Robert Kennedy's children was named after Taylor.

12. A group of naval officers who opposed the decision by Secretary of Defense Louis Johnson to cancel the construction of the supercarrier, the *United States,* after the keel had been laid challenged the Secretary's decision in the press and in public speeches. The episode has been dubbed the "Revolt of the Admirals."

13. Taylor, *Trumpet,* p. 175.

14. Elmo Zumwalt, *On Watch* (New York: Quadrangle, 1976), p. 316.

15. Ibid.

16. Ibid., p. 314.

17. Ibid., p. 295.

18. Richard Nixon, *The Memoirs of Richard Nixon* (New York: Grosset and Dunlap, 1978), pp. 447, 498.

19. Ibid., p. 457.

20. Zumwalt, *On Watch,* pp. 570-71; Nixon, *Memoirs,* p. 528.

21. Quoted in "Gen. Brown's Political Myopia," *Washington Post,* March 29, 1977, p. A14.

22. Brown's views are contained in his *United States Military Posture for FY 1976, FY 1977, FY 1978 and FY 1979.*

23. Zumwalt, *On Watch,* p. 441. The former CNO notes that he does not share this opinion but can understand it.

24. William Watts and Lloyd Free, "State of the Nation III" (Washington, D.C.: Potomac Associates, July 1978).

25. "Gen. Brown's Political Myopia."

26. Westmoreland argues his own case in *A Soldier Reports* (Garden City, N.Y.: Doubleday, 1976). The former Vietnam commander insists that the military still could have won the war if it had not been for the meddling of civilian policy makers.

27. Zumwalt, *On Watch,* p. 296.

28. Abrams's performance in that situation was so impressive that Secretary of the Army Cyrus Vance wanted him named as Army Chief of Staff in 1962 even though Abrams was only a two-star general.

29. *The Pentagon Papers* are filled with predictions by high-ranking officers referring to "light at the end of the tunnel." Neil Sheehan, *The Pentagon Papers* (New York: Bantam Books, 1971).

30. Zumwalt's years as CNO are recounted in his *On Watch*.

31. Ibid., p. 478.

32. "Interview with Admiral James L. Holloway III," *U.S. News and World Report*, October 20, 1975, pp. 61-64.

33. James Holloway, "The Transition to V/STOL," *Naval Institute Proceedings*, September 1977, pp. 19-24.

34. Edward Kolodiej, *The Uncommon Defense and Congress* (Columbus: Ohio State University Press, 1965), pp. 411-17.

35. Data on the extent of Marine Corps participation in JCS matters was furnished by Headquarters, Marine Corps.

36. Richard Betts, *Soldiers, Statesmen and Cold War Crises* (Cambridge, Mass.: Harvard University Press, 1977), pp. 179-80.

37. Ibid., p. 119.

38. Westmoreland, *A Soldier Reports*, pp. 343-44.

39. Commandants of the Marine Corps are not included in this number because the Marines do not have their own academy; it is the exception rather than the rule for Commandants to be service academy graduates.

40. Zumwalt, *On Watch*, p. 24.

CHAPTER 5

Beyond Vietnam: Détente and the Emerging Consensus

Through the leadership of Secretaries of Defense Laird and Schlesinger and the JCS, the Department of Defense took a number of steps which helped the Pentagon successfully adjust to the environment of the 1969-1974 period. However, at the beginning of 1975, there was still a great deal of uneasiness among the military hierarchy. This was caused by two factors. First, détente seemed to be creating more problems for the Pentagon than it solved; second, the American political system had not yet achieved a firm consensus on the type of defense force it wanted to support. In real terms, the defense budget was still declining although not as steeply, and it was not yet clear where it would bottom out. It is important to examine the way in which these two phenomena, détente and the attitude of the American people toward defense, impacted on the fortunes of the Pentagon in the 1975-1978 time frame.

Détente

From the viewpoint of the Pentagon, détente and all that it implies proved to be a mixed blessing. On the one hand, the new relationship between the United States and the Soviet Union allowed the two superpowers to conclude several mutually beneficial agreements in the area of strategic weaponry. In contrast, the feeling that the Soviet Union and this country were entering a period of decreased tensions made it difficult for the Pentagon to persuade Congress and the American people that "détente without defense" is delusion. The following is a detailed examination of the positive and negative aspects of détente from the Pentagon's perspective.

Strategic Arms Limitation

Strategic arms limitations talks (SALT) between the United States and the Soviet Union were begun in earnest in the fall of 1969.[1] The first phase of SALT (or SALT I) culminated in May 1972 when the two superpowers concluded two major agreements: an antiballistic missile (ABM) treaty and an interim agreement on offensive systems. The ABM treaty restricted both sides to no more than two ABM sites, with no more than one hundred launchers permitted at each site. The interim agreement froze for five years the number of land-based intercontinental ballistic missiles (ICBMs) and sea-launched ballistic missiles (SLBMs) at the level existing or under construction as of May 1972. Under the terms of the pact, the United States was restricted to a combination of 1,710 missiles while the Soviets were limited to 2,280 land- and sea-based missiles. Neither the number of warheads on each missile nor the number of intercontinental bombers was affected by the interim agreement.

On November 21, 1972, the United States and the Soviet Union opened negotiations to replace the interim agreement with a more comprehensive and long-term treaty on strategic offensive systems. As of early 1979, the two sides had not yet completely achieved this goal. However, they had reached three agreements which moved them toward that objective. In a summit meeting in Washington in the summer of 1973, President Nixon and Chairman Brezhnev agreed on Basic Principles of Negotiations to guide the SALT II discussions. The following summer in Moscow, the two leaders decided to amend the ABM treaty in order to limit ABM deployment to one instead of two sites per side and pledged themselves to negotiate a more comprehensive pact on strategic offensive weapons which would follow the interim agreement and run until 1985. Finally, in a summit meeting in Vladivostok in October 1974, newly installed President Gerald Ford and Chairman Brezhnev concluded a new agreement. The Ford-Brezhnev pact, or Vladivostok accord, limited each side to an aggregate of 2,400 strategic delivery systems of any type, that is, ICBMs, SLBMs, and heavy bombers, and to an aggregate of 1,320 missiles with multiple warheads (MIRVs).

SALT/Savings

The most obvious advantage of the SALT agreements for the Pentagon has been monetary savings. If the United States had been forced to build a complete twenty-six-site ABM system, the total cost would have been in excess of $100 billion. The cost of building the one ABM site at Grand Forks, Montana, came to $6 billion. Moreover, without the SALT I and Vladivostok agreements, the United States would have had to increase its strategic offensive spending dramatically. As is indicated in Table 30, the interim agreement has kept the Soviet Union some 25 percent below its projected levels. Under its constraints the Soviet force has 820 fewer missiles,

Table 30   U.S./USSR Strategic Forces and the Interim Agreement

| Category | Without Interim Agreement | | Under Interim Agreement | | Change | | | |
| | | | | | N | | % | |
	USSR	US	USSR	US	USSR	US	USSR	US
ICBMs	1900	1054	1330	1054	-570	0	-30	0
SLBMs	1200	656	950	656	-250	0	-21	0
Warheads	3400	11000	2600	11000	-800	0	-24	0
Megatonnage	5500	4500	4000	4450	-1500	-50	-27	1

Source: Alton Quanbeck and Barry Blechman, "The Arms Accords: Everyone Gains," *Washington Post*, June 20, 1972, p. B1.

800 less warheads, and 1,500 fewer megatons than projected. Likewise, the Vladivostok agreement, by putting a limit on the number of missiles which can be "mirved," has kept the Soviet Union from exploiting completely its throw-weight advantage and forging ahead of the United States in the number of warheads. Although it is hard to put a precise price tag on the money saved in the area of strategic offensive arms, there have been some indications of its magnitude. In June 1973, President Nixon stated that without SALT I, he would have had to request $15 billion more for defense in FY 1973 alone.[2] In August 1975, President Ford spoke of spending an additional $2-$3 billion on strategic weapons if the SALT talks collapsed.[3] That same month, Secretary of Defense Schlesinger argued that the United States would have to spend $8-$10 billion additional over the 1975-1980 period if the SALT talks did not make meaningful progress.[4] In January 1976, Secretary of Defense Donald Rumsfeld stated that if the United States and the Soviet Union did not work out a SALT II agreement, the Pentagon would need a large increase in its budget.

Rumsfeld revealed that a special group within the National Security Council had worked out a "no SALT budget."[5]

In January 1978, Congressman Les Aspin (D-Wis.) estimated that without a SALT II agreement, the United States will have to increase defense spending by $20 billion just to stay even with the Soviets.[6]

Problem Areas

The Pentagon hierarchy was grateful that the SALT I and Vladivostok agreements spared them the painful choice of either spending large sums on strategic systems or allowing our strategic position vis-à-vis the Soviets to deteriorate. However, there are several aspects of the SALT agreements that trouble both the civilian and military leaders within DOD. These problem areas fall into three categories.

First, because the interim and Vladivostok agreements do not permit either side to increase the size of its missiles, they lock this country into a permanent position of inferiority in regard to missile throw-weight, or the lifting capacity of its missile force. Thus, when the Soviets achieve the United States' level of warhead design sophistication, their strategic forces will be able to carry four times the number of warheads as United States missiles. Second, the Vladivostok agreement does not consider the Soviet's new long-range bomber, the Backfire, a heavy bomber. Thus, this plane does not count toward the Soviet ceiling on strategic delivery systems. However, the United States must count all of its B-52s against the 2,400 delivery systems which each side is allowed. In the view of many Pentagon leaders, the Backfire should be considered a strategic weapon because it can attack this country. For example, a Backfire based in the Chukotsk Peninsula of Northeast Siberia would be capable, in a round-trip subsonic flight without refueling, of reaching targets in the United States from southern California to the eastern tip of Lake Superior. On a one-way subsonic flight without refueling, it would be capable of attacking targets anywhere in the United States and then flying on to Cuba. With refueling, the Pentagon estimates that the Backfire would be able to reach any target in this country and return to the Soviet Union.[7]

Third, many military officials feel that since the accords have been signed, the Soviet Union has been violating the spirit, if not the letter, of the interim and Vladivostok agreements. In testimony before the House Select Committee on Intelligence on December 2, 1975, Admiral Elmo Zumwalt, the former Chief of Naval Operations, accused the Soviets of gross violations of the interim agreement. As evidence, critics such as Zumwalt point to the following data. The Soviets have built ABM radars in the Kamchatka area of the north-eastern part of the USSR and are transforming antiaircraft missiles throughout the Soviet Union into antiballistic missiles. They are doing this in spite of the fact that the agreements limit the Soviet Union to one ABM site in the Moscow area. In addition, the Russians have replaced about 100 of their light SS-11 missiles with the much larger SS-19s, despite the fact that the interim agreement stipulates that light missiles cannot be replaced by heavier ones. Moreover, since 1972 the Soviets have built at least 150 silos the precise size of SS-18 missile silos and equipped them with launcher-type suspension systems. The SALT I agreement provides that neither side may build new fixed-based intercontinental missile launchers. Furthermore, the Soviets have made extensive use of decoys, encrypted data, and camouflage to interfere with our efforts to verify their strategic strength. Finally, and perhaps most impor-tantly, the Soviets have violated the whole spirit or intent of the SALT agreements by continuing to pursue an aggressive program of building up their strategic forces. Although the Russians have not yet exceeded the upper limits set forth in SALT I, their aggressive building campaign violates the underlying spirit of the entire negotia-tions, namely, that there should be nuclear parity between the two superpowers.[8]

The Soviet Buildup

Although some of the asymetries in the strategic area concern Pentagon policy makers, their real fear is the rapid expansion of the entire Soviet military structure made possible by the continuing high levels of Soviet defense expenditures which have occurred despite the emergence of détente. The Soviet buildup dates to the Cuban missile crisis where a preponderance of American strategic and conventional forces compelled the Soviet Union to withdraw its intermediate range ballistic missiles from Cuba. After this humiliation, the Soviet leadership was determined never again to be placed in a situation where they had to back down. Therefore, beginning in the mid-1960s, the Kremlin began to increase its defense expenditures quite rapidly, and by 1968 it had surpassed the United States in defense outlays for the first time in its history. As is indicated in Table 31, from 1963 through 1967 United States defense expenditures were about 10 percent higher than those of the Russians. Between 1968, the time that the Soviets "crossed over," and 1973 the Russians outspent this country by over 20 percent, more than making up for the United States' advantage in the 1963-1967 period.

Most analysts felt that with the signing of the SALT I accords and the coming of détente, Soviet defense expenditures would slow down. However, this did not prove to be the case. In fact, Soviet defense expenditures increased more rapidly after SALT than before, and the gap between the levels of defense expenditures in the United States and the USSR widened even farther. As indicated in Table 32, in the four years immediately preceding SALT I the size of the Soviet defense budget grew by 35 percent and the Russians spent $60 billion, or 21 percent, more than the United States on defense. However, in the 1972-1976 period, Soviet defense expenditures increased by more than 65 percent; the amount they spent on defense was $117 billion, or 28 percent more than the United States. The higher defense figure for the Soviets becomes even more significant when one considers the fact that the Soviets have very low manpower costs and many of their defense expenditures are subsumed in other parts of the Russian bureaucracy. The Soviets spend 30 to 35 percent of their total defense budget on manpower costs. In contrast, the United States must allocate almost 60 percent of its defense budget to manpower. Thus, the Soviets are able to spend nearly twice as much as this country on the investment portions of the budget, that is, weapons procurement, research and development, and such areas as combat training.

The increasing disparity between Soviet and American expenditures in investment has markedly tipped the military balance between the two countries. As is indicated in Table 33, in 1964, as this nation prepared to embark on its Vietnam misadventure, it was far ahead of the Soviet Union in every major category of weapons system. The

Table 31 U.S./USSR Outlays for Defense, 1963-1973 (in billions of dollars)

	Calendar Year												
	1963	1964	1965	1966	1967	1968	1969	1970	1971	1972	1973	Total	Average
U.S.[1]	52	51	52	58	55	53	52	54	60	69	72	628	57
USSR	47	47	46	48	52	60	64	69	74	81	86	674	61
Difference	+5	+4	+6	+10	+3	-7	-12	-15	-14	-12	-14	-46	-4
%	+9.6	+7.8	+11.5	+17.2	+5.4	-13.2	-23.1	-27.7	-23.3	-17.4	-19.4	-7.0	-7.0

1. Excludes outlays for war in Southeast Asia.

Sources: Arms Control and Disarmament Agency, *World Military Expenditures and Arms Trade, 1963-1973*, and Melvin Laird, *Annual Defense Department Report, FY 1973*, February 17, 1972, p. 33.

Table 32   U.S./USSR Outlays for Defense, 1968-1976

Pre-Salt I	Calendar Year					Total	Change 1968-1972	
	1968	1969	1970	1971	1972	1968-1972	N	%
U.S.[1]	53	52	54	60	69	288	16	30.2
USSR	60	64	69	74	81	348	21	35.0
Difference	-7	-12	-15	-14	-12	60		
%	-13.2	-23.1	-27.7	-23.3	-17.4	-20.8		

Post Salt I						Total	Change 1972-1976	
	1972	1973	1974	1975	1976	1972-1976	N	%
U.S.[1]	69	78	86	91	94	418	25	36.3
USSR	81	95	106	119	134	535	53	65.4
Difference	-12	-17	-20	-28	-40	-117		
%	-17.4	-21.7	-23.2	-30.7	42.5	-27.9		

1. Excludes outlays for the war in Southeast Asia.

Source: Arms Control and Disarmament Agency, *World Military Expenditures and Arms Transfers 1967-66*, and *Arms Control 1977*.

Table 33 U.S./USSR Force Levels for Selected Calendar Years

System	1964		1968		1972		1976		Change N		Change %	
	U.S.	USSR	U.S.	USSR	U.S.	USSR	U.S.	USSR	U.S.	USSR	U.S.	USSR
ICBMs	654	200	1054	700	1054	1118	1054	1527	400	1327	61	664
SLBMs	336	20	656	50	656	450	656	845	320	825	95	4125
Bombers	630	190	650	250	569	140	387	140	-243	-50	-39	-26
Major Surface Combatant Ships	300	200	325	200	250	225	175	225	-125	25	-42	13
Tactical Aircraft	5700	3500	5700	3500	5000	4500	5000	6000	-700	2500	-12	71
Division Equivalents[1]	19	7	20	10	16	25	16	25	-3	18	-16	255

1. U.S. and Soviet divisions are not directly comparable. Soviet divisions are made equivalent to the U.S. in this comparison.

Source: *United States Military Posture* and *Reports of the Secretary of Defense* (for selected years).

United States had 770 more or nearly five times as many land- and sea-based missiles as the Soviet Union, more than three times as many long-range bombers, 100 more combatant ships, 2,200 more tactical aircraft, and nearly three times as many Army and Marine divisions. Four years later, the Soviets began to close the gap. By 1972, the Russians had drawn even with us and by 1976 they were ahead of the United States in every major category of weapon system except long-range bombers. In that year, the Soviets had 662 more missiles than this nation. They had 50 more major surface combatant ships, about 1,000 more tactical aircraft, and 60 percent more ground divisions. In 1976, the United States had 2 million men under arms while the Soviet Union possessed an armed force of more than 4 million. Moreover, given the present output rates of the Soviet Union as compared to those of the United States, the situation will continue to worsen for the Pentagon. The Soviets are now outproducing the United States by about 3 to 1 in major weapons programs. Annually, the Russians turn out about 3,000 tanks, 930 tactical aircraft, 39 surface ships, and 10 submarines. Corresponding figures for the United States are 540 tanks, 540 tactical aircraft, 11 surface ships, and 3 submarines.[9]

This remarkable growth of Soviet armed strength has not been without its impact in the international area. For example, during the October 1973 war in the Middle East, Soviet warships in the Mediterranean outnumbered United States ships 98 to 65. Moreover, the Russians could have attacked the U.S. Sixth Fleet with land-based aircraft flying in from four directions—Egypt, Syria, the Crimean, and Yugoslavia. According to Admiral Zumwalt, the CNO in 1973, it was this Soviet superiority that forced us to yield to the savage Soviet ultimatum that the United States force the Israelis to allow the entrapped Egyptian Third Army to escape.[10]

Similarly, many analysts feel that the United States cannot win a conventional war against the Soviets in Europe. For example, Drew Middleton, the *New York Times* military correspondent, argues that the United States and its NATO allies lack both the weapons and the troops to hold off the Soviets and their Warsaw Pact allies. As is indicated in Table 34, in 1976, the Warsaw Pact had some 203,000 more troops, over 9,000 more tanks, and some 1,700 more tactical aircraft than NATO. In view of this disparity, it is not surprising that

Table 34   NATO and Warsaw Pact Forces Deployed in Central Europe in 1976

	NATO	Warsaw Pact	Difference N	Difference %
Troops	732,000	935,000	203,000	28
Main Battle Tanks	6,730	16,200	9,470	141
Tactical Aircraft	1,334	3,075	1,741	131

Source: Adapted from International Institute for Strategic Studies, *Military Balance, 1977-1978.*

Middleton concluded that the Communist forces would easily push the Western troops as far west as the English Channel and south through France perhaps to the Spanish frontier. The outlook would be for a short, hard-hitting conventional war that the West, in the circumstances which prevailed in 1976, could not win.[11]

In spite of the rapid Soviet buildup, their continued high level of defense expenditures, and the pessimistic prognostications about the military situation by such obervers as Zumwalt and Middleton, the Pentagon well into 1976 still found it difficult to convince the American public to support higher defense expenditures. However, the civilian and military leaders continued to make their case in public forums. As former Secretary of Defense Schlesinger noted, "If we are to maintain a position of power, the public must be informed about the trends. Some years from now, somebody will raise the question, why were we not warned, and I want to be able to say indeed you were."[12]

Yet in an era of détente, it was difficult to make a convincing case that the Soviets in fact posed a greater threat than they did in the dark days of the Cold War. The Pentagon may have felt that détente without defense was delusion, but in the mid-1970s to many it sounded like alarmism on the part of the military. The overall Pentagon position on détente with the Soviet Union, which its leaders attempted to convey to the public, was summarized succinctly in a document prepared by the Defense Intelligence Agency (DIA) and entitled "Détente in Soviet Strategy." According to this study, détente is a gambit that the Russians are using in order to facilitate their objective of attaining ultimate overall dominance of the West. This dominance would include the breakup of the Western alliances, the eviction of the American military from Europe and the achievement of Soviet dominance there, and the establishment of Soviet political, military, technological, and economic superiority worldwide.

The Soviets feel that they can achieve this domination because détente has given them the following advantages: a strategic posture vis-à-vis the United States that diminishes the likelihood of general nuclear war and a steady development of Soviet conventional military capabilities concurrent with a trend in the West to reduce general-purpose force strengths; a political environment in which they can win substantial concessions on arms control and security; the recognition of the Soviet Union's World War II gains in Europe; freer access to Western food, trade and technology; and a growing dismay and disunity in the West on strategic policy and security matters.[13]

However, in mid-1975, almost without warning, a new consensus began to emerge on the need to enhance our military posture. Soviet actions played a part in this reversal of public opinion. Most of those who are normally skeptical of Pentagon claims concerning the Soviet military began to wonder what motivated the Russians. Neither the duration nor the extent of the Soviet buildup could be justified by considerations of defense alone. Even these skeptics could no longer ignore the massive Soviet arsenal, their pushing of the SALT agreements to their absolute limits, Russian aid to the militant factions in the Middle East, and, finally, Soviet involvement throughout the African continent. By the time of the 1976 presidential campaign, incumbent President Gerald Ford found himself being attacked by Ronald Reagan, his Republican challenger in the primaries, and Jimmy Carter, his Democratic contestant in the general election, for not doing enough to combat the Soviets.[14]

However, it was not the Soviet actions alone which triggered the new American attitude toward defense. Indeed, Soviet behavior remained consistent. Rather, two events which occurred in the spring of 1975 allowed the people of this nation to once again take an objective and unemotional look at the military balance and the role of military force as an instrument of policy—the final collapse of the non-Communist governments of South Vietnam and Cambodia and the seizure of the merchant ship *Mayaguez*. These events prepared the way for the new consensus and a rise in the fortunes of the Pentagon.

The New Consensus

In February 1973, the United States officially ended its direct involvement in South Vietnam when it signed the Paris Peace Accords. In return for the release of its prisoners of war, this nation agreed to withdraw its remaining combat troops from Vietnam. This completed a process which had begun in the spring of 1969 when President Nixon announced the first troop withdrawals. Although the United States withdrew the last of its fighting men from Southeast Asia in early 1973, it was still financially and psychologically committed to the support of the Thieu regime in South Vietnam and the Lon Nol government in Cambodia. Military aid to Southeast Asia in FY 1974 was $1.8 billion and for FY 1975 it was projected to be $1.4 billion. Moreover, as long as our involvement in Southeast Asia remained, the American political system could not seem to complete the post-Vietnam adjustment. The nation appeared to be poised between the two poles of world policeman and isolationism, unable to decide in which direction to move. Indeed, President Nixon and Secretary of State Kissinger clung to the decadent, but non-Communist, regimes in Southeast Asia because they feared that a precipitous abandonment of these allies could spark a wave of neo-isolationism in this country.[15]

Most objective analysts felt that eventually the Communists would be victorious in Southeast Asia. They were better organized, more disciplined, and less corrupt than any of the other forces in the region. However, few felt that the end would come as suddenly as it did. Almost without warning, the situation became unraveled in Cambodia and South Vietnam. In early 1975, it appeared that the struggles would go on for several more years at least. But by the end of April it was all over. "May Day" 1975 saw the National Liberation Front in power in Saigon and the Khmer Rouge holding forth in Pnom Phen.

Initially, it seemed that the spring 1975 debacle in Southeast Asia might cause recriminations that would tear this country apart and possibly provoke an isolationist reaction. At first, Secretary of Defense Schlesinger blamed the fall of Saigon on congressional niggardliness and Vice President Rockefeller stated that Congress would have to answer to the public for allowing South Vietnam to collapse. However, cooler heads quickly prevailed. Schlesinger recanted his statement, which put the blame on Congress, and President Ford told the American people that they must put Vietnam behind them.[16]

The real end of our twenty-five-year involvement in Southeast Asia did not provoke an isolationist reaction. Rather, it seemed to clear the air so that a badly needed new consensus on national security policy could emerge. The new consensus seemed to coalesce around the following points. The United States could no longer fiscally or psychologically afford to be the world's policeman. A quarter of a century of bearing this burden had drained our economic and emotional resources. Nor in the era of détente was there any real need for this nation to fulfill this role. However, the United States could not retreat to neo-isolationism. It is a world power with concrete definable interests in the international arena which cannot be supported without a strong military force. Moreover, not only must this military force be strong, it must be perceived as strong by the rest of the world. As one commentator so aptly put it, "Like it or not, American military power does defend open societies in Europe. It enables Israel to keep its head above water and Japan not to rearm. It gives Communist China a reason for not making a settlement with Russia on Moscow's terms."[17]

The importance of having a wide range of military options was dramatically demonstrated within a fortnight of the collapse in Southeast Asia. On May 12, 1975, the new Cambodian government boarded an unarmed American merchant vessel, the freighter *Mayaguez*, and removed its crew. To rescue the crew, the Ford administration found it necessary to launch air strikes against military and fuel installations on the Cambodian mainland and conduct an amphibious operation against a Cambodian-occupied island. Although the operation was poorly handled by the Pentagon, and forty-one servicemen were killed in rescuing thirty-nine crewmen, the use of military force was overwhelmingly supported by the American public.[18] President Ford's approval rating with the

American public jumped by more than 11 percentage points as a result of his handling of the crisis. Just as the collapse in Southeast Asia had signaled the end of an era in which the United States had been the world's policeman, the *Mayaguez* incident appeared to mark the beginning of a new period in which this nation would rely on a strong military to safeguard its own interests.

Pentagon spokesmen had been arguing throughout the entire 1969-1975 period that this nation needed a strong military force. However, it was not until the collapse of Vietnam and the *Mayaguez* seizure that the political system was able to develop a consensus on this point. The events in Southeast Asia narrowed the gap between the perceptions of the public and the Pentagon. This new congruence can be demonstrated through a comparison of the defense budgets in the latter half of the 1970s to those of the first half.

In the FY 1970-75 period, defense authority rose from $76.1 billion to $89 billion, a total increase of $12.9 billion, or 16.9 percent, or an average of 3.4 percent annually. During that same period, outlays for DOD increased by just under $7 billion, or 9 percent, or an average annual increase of only 1.8 percent. In constant FY 1975 dollars, authority actually decreased by about $18 billion, or 16.6 percent, and outlays by almost $25 billion, or 22.3 percent. It would have cost almost $110 billion in FY 1975 dollars to fund the defense budget of FY 1970. The Pentagon's share of the GNP and total federal budget also declined rapidly during the FY 1970-1975 time frame. The DOD's portion of the GNP dipped by an average of .5 percentage points each year and the Pentagon's share of the total federal budget dropped by almost 15 percentage points. These trends in defense spending in the FY 1970-1975 period are summarized in Table 35.

However, with its FY 1976 defense budget the Pentagon sought to reverse these downward trends in a dramatic fashion. In this budget, which was presented to the Congress in early 1975, the Pentagon broke the symbolic threshold of $100 billion for the first time by requesting $104.7 billion in TOA. The DOD sought to increase authority by approximately 18 percent and outlays by 10 percent above their FY 1975 levels. Moreover, as Secretary Schlesinger noted in presenting the FY 1976 budget to Congress, it would lay the foundation for real increases in defense spending for the remainder of the decade.[19] As indicated in Table 36, by FY 1980 defense

Table 35 Trends in Defense Spending, FY 1970 to FY 1975 (in billions of dollars)

| | Fiscal Year | | | | | | Change 1970-1975 | | Average Change, % |
	1970	1971	1972	1973	1974	1975	N	%	
Current									
TOA	76.1	74.6	77.7	80.9	85.0	89.0	12.9	16.9	3.4
Outlays	77.9	74.5	75.8	74.8	78.4	84.8	6.9	8.9	1.8
Constant[1]									
TOA	106.7	97.4	96.3	92.2	93.0	89.0	-17.7	-16.6	-3.3
Outlays	109.2	97.3	93.9	85.7	85.8	84.8	-24.4	-22.3	-4.5
% GNP	8.0	7.2	6.9	6.2	5.8	5.9	-2.1	-2.6	-0.5
% Federal Budget	40.8	35.5	31.7	29.0	28.2	26.1	-14.7	-26.0	-7.2

1. In Fy 1975 dollars.

Sources: *The Budgets of the United States Government, FY 1970-1975* and *Annual Department of Defense Reports, FY 1970-1975.*

Table 36 TOA and Outlays in the Defense Budget, FY 1975 to FY 1980 (in billions of current dollars)

Fiscal Year	TOA	Outlays by Fiscal Year							
		1975	1976	197T³	1977	1978	1979	1980	Later
(prior balance)¹		22.6	9.2	1.5	3.5	1.8	1.0	.3	6.6
1975	89.0	62.2	14.4	2.2	4.4	2.2	.8	.4	2.3
1976	104.7		69.2	6.7	15.7	5.7	2.9	1.0	3.5
197T	24.6			15.0	4.7	3.2	1.0	.4	.5
1977	116.6				75.7	23.5	8.8	4.0	4.6
1978	127.8					82.6	26.2	9.5	9.5
1979	138.3						89.3	28.7	20.3
1980	147.9							95.6	52.3
Total Outlays		84.8	92.8	25.4	104.0	119.0	130.0	140.0	99.7

1. TOA remaining from prior to FY 1975.
2. Uses inflation assumptions of the Office of Management and Budget (OMB). Average inflation rate in 1975-1980 period is 6.5 percent.
3. 197T refers to the transitional period from July through September 1976, when the start of the fiscal year was changed from July 1 to October 1.

Source: Assistant Secretary of Defense (Comptroller).

authority would have moved to $147.9 billion and outlays to $140 billion, if the essentials of the FY 1976 program were accepted. This would have represented a total increase of 66 percent above the TOA and outlay levels of FY 1975. In its FY 1976 budget, the Ford administration also sought to reverse the pattern of defense receiving smaller shares of the GNP and the federal budget. As is indicated in Table 37, if the premises of the FY 1976 budget were accepted, defense's share of the GNP would have risen to 6 percent and its portion of the total federal budget would have moved back up to almost 29.3 percent by the end of the decade.

Table 37   Defense Outlays as a Portion of the GNP and the Total Budget, FY 1976 to FY 1980 (in billions of current dollars)

Category	Fiscal Year					
	1976	1977	1978	1979	1980	Average
Defense Outlays	92.8	104	119	130	140	117.2
GNP[1]	1686	1863	2040	2205	2352	2029.2
% GNP	5.5	5.6	5.8	5.9	6.0	5.8
Federal Budget	368	393	425	452	477	423
% Federal Budget	25.6	26.5	28.0	28.8	29.3	27.7

1. Assumes a real growth of 3 percent in GNP.
Sources: *The Budget of the United States Government, FY 1976*, pp. 41-48, and *Annual Defense Department Report, FY 1976 and FY 197T*, p. 126.

There were two other characteristics of the FY 1976 budget that are of significance in discussing the new consensus. First, the driving force behind the upward pressures on future defense budgets would no longer be personnel costs. As was discussed in Chapter 1, personnel costs rose substantially in the post-1968 period. In FY 1968, personnel costs accounted for 43 percent of the defense budget; by FY 1975, the share of defense spending devoted to personnel had risen to 56 percent. However, in the post-1975 period personnel costs would no longer force up defense outlays. In current dollars, personnel costs for FY 1976 were only 5 percent above their FY 1975 level, and in real terms, personnel costs actually declined by $7 billion, or 1.4 percent. The share of the defense budget consumed by personnel costs in FY 1976 dropped to 55 percent, and by FY 1980 the portion of defense outlays devoted to personnel was projected to fall below 50 percent. In the last half of the 1970s, for the first time in a decade, the real impetus behind the projected increase in defense spending was the bigger amounts programmed for investment. Between FY 1975 and FY 1976, DOD sought to increase funds for procurement, R, D, T, and E, and construction by $10 billion, or 36 percent, in current dollars and $7.5 billion, or 24.8 percent, in real terms. By FY 1980, DOD wanted to spend $52.4 billion, or nearly 38 percent, of its total budget on investment. This figure represented an increase of almost $25 billion or 88 percent above the FY 1975 level. The projected reversal in the personnel-investment balance in the FY 1975-1980 period is outlined in Table 38.

Second, despite the size of the increase in the FY 1976 budget and its long-range implications, the Pentagon made no attempt to mask the new upward trends. Secretary of Defense Schlesinger stated bluntly that he made no apologies for the size of the budget. Indeed, in his annual report he attempted to lay out what he perceived as the real choice facing the American people. That is, do we wish to fulfill our responsibilities or do we wish to reduce them. If the people choose the former, the Secretary argued, then they must be willing to support a military establishment strong enough to carry out those responsibilities. According to Schlesinger, we must recognize that there is a strong connection between the safety, interests, commitments, and foreign policy of the United States on the one hand, and the size, composition, and deployment of our defense establishment on the other.[20]

Initially, it seemed that Congress would make the latter choice, that is, reduce our commitments. As a result of the 1974 elections, conducted in the aftermath of Watergate, the Democratic party gained a 2 to 1 majority in both Houses. Moreover, many of the Democrats swept into office were young, quite vocal, and antidefense. Many of them campaigned on platforms that indicated that even the pre-1975 levels of defense spending were already too high. One of the first things that these "angry young men" did was to depose F. Edward Hebert (D-La.), a long-time advocate of a strong defense establishment, as Chairman of the House Armed Services Committee. When the FY 1976 turnaround budget was presented, many of these Congressmen referred to it as a wrong-way budget. They argued that instead of increasing defense spending the federal

Table 38 Functional Breakdown of the Defense Budget, FY 1975, FY 1976, and FY 1980 (in billions of dollars)

	Current Dollars				Current FY 1976 Dollars			
	FY75	FY76	%Change	FY80	FY75	FY76	%Change	FY80
Personnel								
Military	25.0	25.9	3.5		26.5	25.9	-2.3	
Retired	6.3	6.9	9.5		6.6	6.9	4.5	
Civilian	14.6	15.4	5.5		15.8	15.4	-2.5	
Housing	1.2	1.3	8.3		1.3	1.3	0	
TOTAL	47.1	49.5	5.1	66.1	50.2	49.5	-1.4	54.7
Investment								
Procurement	17.4	24.7	42.0		18.8	24.7	31.4	
R, D, T and E	8.6	10.3	19.8		9.3	10.3	10.8	
Construction	1.9	2.9	52.6		2.1	2.9	38.1	
TOTAL	27.9	37.9	35.8	52.4	30.2	37.9	25.5	43.4
O and M	11.7	14.4	23.1	18.5	13.4	14.4	7.5	15.3
Assistance	2.3	2.7	17.4	3.0	2.6	2.7	3.8	2.5
TOTAL DOD	89.0	104.7	17.8	140	96.5	104.7	8.5	116

Sources: Assistant Secretary of Defense (Public Affairs), *FY 1976 Department of Defense Budget*, news release 46-75, February 3, 1975, pp. E7, E8, and *Department of Defense Report, FY 1976 and FY 197T*, p. I26.

government ought to be transferring funds from defense into the area of human resources.

However, by the time the defense budget was ready for a vote, Cambodia and South Vietnam had fallen, the *Mayaguez* had been seized, and the mood in the country and the Congress had changed. Most legislators feared that severe reductions in defense spending might be interpreted by our allies and adversaries as a sign that the United States had lost its nerve and national will in the wake of the Indochina debacle. The reaction of liberal Senator Allan Cranston (D-Calif.) was typical. He stated that before the fall of Cambodia he intended to support massive reductions in the defense structure, including a 250,000-man reduction in United States forces in Europe. Cranston concluded, however, that such an action was "unwise at this time because it might give the impression that the United States is on the run and turning isolationist."[21] Moreover, according to Senator John Stennis (D-Miss.), the *Mayaguez* incident had demonstrated that for the present "no nation was too small, too weak, or too remote to challenge the United States if the proper opportunity presented itself."[22] Therefore, the United States needed a full range of military options to protect its interests.

On the House and Senate floors, legislators beat back amendment after amendment that would have reversed the strategic and conventional innovations in the FY 1976 Ford defense budget. The key elements in that budget were preserved on the order of 3 to 1 in the House and 2 to 1 in the Senate. Although the total reduction made by the Congress was $7.5 billion, or 7 percent, the cuts were more cosmetic than real. About $1.3 billion of the cut was in the request for aid to Vietnam, which was a moot point after April 30, 1975. Another $1 billion was taken from the Navy's shipbuilding program. However, these funds did not affect any ship projects. The Navy had requested the money to cover anticipated contract claims and inflation on ships under construction. As a legislator so aptly put it, "They just put it off, not cut it. We're going to have to come up with more money next year."[23] Congress made a $800 million reduction by refusing to permit the Pentagon to establish a contingency fund which would allow DOD to replace quickly those weapons which might be taken out of stockpiles for overseas sales. Most of the remainder of the cuts were across-the-board reductions in the thousands of line items in the defense budget. Their main effect was to delay production rates and maintenance schedules. Less than $500 million of the cuts terminated programs. Only 10 percent of the entire $7.5 billion reduction had a lasting effect on future budgets.[24]

In its final two defense budgets, FY 1977 and FY 1978, the Ford administration sought to continue its program of reversing the downward trend in defense spending. For the fiscal year beginning on October 1, 1976, the Ford administration requested $113 billion in authority, and for the fiscal year beginning October 1, 1977, it asked for $123 billion. Ford's FY 1978 budget request was $35.2 billion, or 40 percent, above the level of FY 1975.

To the surprise of many people, President Carter continued the Ford program of raising the level of defense expenditures in real terms. Although he campaigned on a platform of reducing defense spending by $5 to $7 billion a year, once in office the new Chief Executive pledged himself to raising the defense budget by 3 percent a year in real terms through FY 1983 and to maintaining the military balance with the Soviet Union. In the first defense budget, FY 1979, Carter requested an increase of $9.4 billion, or 7.9 percent, in authority and $9.9 billion, or 9.4 percent, in outlays. Moreover, as indicated in Table 39, the five-year defense program presented in

Table 39   The Carter Defense Program

	Fiscal Year (billions of dollars)						
	1977	1978	1979	1980	1981	1982	1983
Total Obligational Authority							
Current Dollars	108.3	116.8	126.0	137.2	148.6	160.5	172.7
FY 1979 Prices	122.6	123.7	126.0	129.4	133.0	136.6	140.3
Outlays							
Current Dollars	95.7	105.3	115.2	125.8	136.5	147.9	159.5
FY 1979 Prices	108.8	111.7	115.2	118.7	122.2	125.9	129.6

Source: Harold Brown, *Department of Defense Annual Report, FY 1979*, p. 12.

January 1978 anticipates raising defense authority to $172.7 billion by FY 1983, that is, increasing the total at a rate of 9.5 percent per year over the next five years. The President made this commitment to DOD in spite of the fact that budget realities forced him to reduce many social programs.

The executive branch was not the only part of the government to reverse its attitude toward defense spending. The Congress, which had made significant reductions in the defense budgets during the FY 1970-1976 period, treated the next three budgets much more benignly. It reduced defense budget authority for FY 1977 by $3 billion, or 2.6 percent; in FY 1978, it cut the administration's request for budget authority by $2.8 billion, or 2.3 percent; and in FY 1979, its reduction amounted to only $2.2 billion, or 1.7 percent. Thus, between FY 1977 and FY 1979, the legislature cut defense budget authority by just $8 billion, or 2.2 percent. This compares to reductions of more than 6 percent between FY 1969 and FY 1976. Figure 6 depicts the changing congressional attitude toward defense.

During the second half of the 1970s, there were a number of other indications that a new national consensus had developed concerning the appropriate emphasis on military power and defense spending. For example, on July 9, 1975, the U.S. Conference of Mayors, despite the fact that their cities were hard pressed for funds, refused to endorse a resolution calling for a shift from military to domestic spending.[25] Likewise, the Brookings Institution, which for the most part identifies itself with liberal alternatives to official policy, did not offer any fundamental critique of the FY 1976 through FY 1979 defense budgets. In fact, its review of the FY 1976 defense budget could propose only a $1.9 billion reduction in this nation's first $100 billion defense budget.[26] The next year the Brookings' analysis argued that the defense budget ought to increase.[27]

A survey conducted in 1976 by the Gallup Organization for Potomac Associates discovered that among the general population the military was the most admired of American institutions, and that the Soviet Union was perceived to be as powerful as the United States. Only 29 percent of the people polled by Gallup said that the defense budget was too high. (In 1974, 43 percent said that the defense budget was too high; in 1969, more than half of the people felt that way.)[28] Moreover, a poll completed in 1978 by Opinion Research Corporation found that people who supported an increase in defense spending expressed a willingness to pay more taxes to pay for the increase.[29] Longtime Pentagon critic Senator William Proxmire (D-Wis.) stated that DOD had solved enormous problems by "wise management and sound decisionmaking";[30] a study group

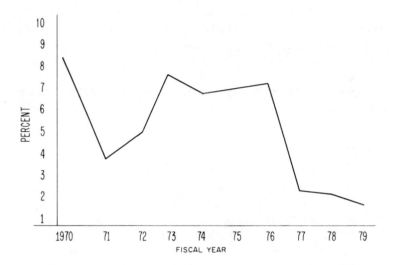

Figure 6 Congressional Reductions in Defense Budget Authority, FY 1970 to FY 1979. Source: Congressional Budget Office, *Budget Storekeeping Reports* **(appropriate years).**

commissioned by President Carter to review the department's operations concluded that on the whole it is well managed.[31]

Certain conditions in the domestic environment have also helped the Pentagon overcome its problems. For example, the nation's continuing high unemployment rate among its youth has enabled DOD to make the transition from a conscripted to an all-volunteer force (AVF) quite successfully. Their services are not only meeting their quotas in the draft-free environment, but the mental capacity of the new recruits is at its highest level in history. In FY 1976, the percentage of high school graduates joining the service was 80 percent. A decade ago, only 65 percent of the recruits had completed high school. The percentage of new recruits in the below-average mental category is only 8 percent, the lowest since DOD began keeping records in 1951. In addition, the Pentagon has assembled a force which is reasonably representative of the racial and regional composition of the nation.[32]

Conclusion

Barring any major changes in the international environment, it seems safe to predict that the defense posture of this nation has been set for the next decade. The United States has apparently decided that it must attempt to support its commitments in Europe, Japan, and the Middle East until the Soviet Union accepts the permanency and legitimacy of Western social order. Support of these commitments will require that this nation spend increasing sums on defense each year. The Pentagon will try to maintain a force of 2 million active duty servicemen and women capable of providing a backdrop for the conduct of American diplomacy and applying force across the entire spectrum of conventional warfare, that is, from *Mayaguez* incidents to the protection of NATO. The DOD will continue to attempt to maintain essential equivalence with the Soviet Union in the area of strategic nuclear forces by increasing the accuracy and yield of its missiles and bombers. It appears this force will enable the United States to play the role that it wishes in the international arena and will provide fairness and balance between national security and other pressing needs. However, it does not mean that the Pentagon has solved all of its problems. A number of challenges confront the Pentagon as it enters the decade of the 1980s.

Notes

1. For a good summary of the SALT negotiations, see the following: "SALT: The Vladivostok Summit 1974," *U.S. Department of State*, January 1975; Richard Nixon, *Memoirs of Richard Nixon* (New York: Grosset and Dunlap, 1978), pp. 609-21; and Marvin Kalb and Bernard Kalb, *Kissinger* (Boston: Little, Brown, 1974), pp. 312-35.

2. George Wilson, "SALT Forestalls Rise in Budget, Nixon Says," *Washington Post*, June 1972, pp. 4, 6.

3. "The High Cost of SALT," *Newsweek*, September 1, 1975, p. 5.

4. Ibid.

5. Donald Rumsfeld, *Annual Defense Department Report FY 1977*, January 26, 1976, p. 61.

6. George Wilson, "Aspin Sees $20 Billion Savings in SALT II," *Washington Post*, January 9, 1978, p.2.

7. John Finney, "A U.S. Cruise Missile and a Soviet Bomber," *New York Times*, December 14, 1975, p.1.

8. For a listing of alleged Soviet violations, see Elmo Zumwalt, "Learning from Arms Talks with the Soviets," *New York Times*, January 21, 1976, p.27.

9. *Armed Forces Journal*, January 1976, p. 4.

10. George C. Wilson, "Soviet Navy Plans Better Than U.S., Zumwalt Says," *Washington Post*, July 28, 1975, p. A1., and Elmo Zumwalt, *On Watch* (New York: Quadrangle, 1976), p. 448.

11. Drew Middleton, *Can America Win Another War?* (New York: Scribners, 1975).

12. Quoted in George Wilson, "Schlesinger Warns of Illusions," *Washington Post*, November 11, 1975, p. A8.

13. The study is summarized in David Binder, "Pentagon Voices Doubt on Detente," *New York Times*, October 9, 1975, p.5.

14. For a good analysis of this situation, see Martin Schram, *Running for President 1976* (New York: Stein and Day, 1978), pp. 269-70.

15. For an explanation of this phenomenon see Marvin Kalb and Bernard Kalb, *Kissinger*, pp. 120-85, and Richard Nixon, *Memoirs*, pp. 404-20.

16. Carrol Kilpatrick, "Ford Calls Alliances Strong, Firm," *Washington Post*, June 5, 1975, p. A1.

17. Joseph Kraft, "Debating Defense," *Washington Post*, June 3, 1975, p. A19.

18. Charles Miller, the captain of the *Mayaguez*, told a House International Relations Subcommittee that the use of force by the United States was crucial. According to Miller, it was not until U.S. warplanes appeared over Cambodia that the Khmer Rouge began to discuss freeing his men

(*Washington Post*, July 26, 1975, p. A6). The General Accounting Office came to the opposite conclusion; that is, that the Cambodians had begun releasing the crew before the bombing and assault began.

19. James Schlesinger, *Annual Defense Department Report, FY 1976 and FY 1977*, February 5, 1975, p. I-1-2.

20. Ibid.

21. Senator Allan Cranston (D-Calif.) made these remarks on the Senate Floor, June 4, 1975.

22. Spencer Rich, "Weapons Debate Shows Senate Split," *Washington Post*, June 3, 1975, p. A2.

23. Congressman Les Aspin (D-Wis.), quoted in Michael Getler, "Pentagon Budget Slashed," *Washington Post*, May 7, 1975, p. A1. Congress eventually came up with over $2 billion in 1978 to pay for the shipbuilding claims.

24. Barry Blechman and Edward Fried, "Controlling the Defense Budget," *Foreign Affairs*, January 1976, pp. 240-41.

25. David Broder, "Mayors' East Defense Stance," *Washington Post*, July 10, 1975, p. A2.

26. Barry Blechman et. al., *Setting National Priorities, The 1976 Budget* (Washington, D.C.: Brookings Institution, 1975), p. 148.

27. Henry Owen and Charles Schultze et al., *Setting National Priorities: The Next Ten Years* (Washington, D.C.: Brookings Institution, 1976), p. 127.

28. William Watts and Lloyd Free, *State of the Nation III* (Washington, D.C.: Potomac Associates, 1978).

29. The results of this poll are reported in Rowland Evans and Robert Novak, "Nation's Mood Appears to Favor Bigger Defense Spending," *Providence Journal*, March 8, 1978, p.20.

30. William Proxmire, Senate speech, April 29, 1974. Quoted in the *Washington Post*, April 30, 1974, p. 1.

31. Paul Ignatius, *Departmental Headquarters Study*, June 1, 1978.

32. George Wilson, "Quality Youths Enlisting," *Washington Post*, January 3, 1976, p. A1, and Pentagon news briefing by William Brehm, Assistant Secretary of Defense for Manpower and Reserve Affairs, February 13, 1975.

CHAPTER 6

Unsolved
Problems

From the point of view of the Pentagon, today's world is vastly different from that of 1968. The American military has now gone through the agony of adjustment to post-Vietnam realities. Many of the problems that confronted the Pentagon at the end of the last decade have been solved or overcome. The all-volunteer force has become a reality, and despite a declining male population it continues to meet its goals. The war in Southeast Asia is finally behind us and antiwar demonstrations on our college campuses are no more. The downward trend in defense spending has been reversed and the nation appears to have achieved a consensus on the priority to be given defense needs. Great care is taken in selecting the hierarchy of the Pentagon; consequently, civilian and military leadership in the Department of Defense is uniformly high and civil-military relations at the policy-making level are relatively harmonious. The weapons systems operated by our armed forces have been modernized. Reenlistment rates are satisfactory, morale is relatively good, drug and race problems have abated. Defense management practices have improved and cost overruns attributed to shoddy management have gone down. The military has regained its prestige among the American public. Poll after poll shows it to be the most admired institution. Finally, as a result of Soviet actions and the withdrawal of the United States from Southeast Asia, there is a consensus that a successful foreign policy requires a strong military component.

However, the Pentagon has by no means solved all of its problems. As it looks toward the last twenty years of this century, the Department of Defense confronts a new set of challenges. Although not all of these are of the Pentagon's own making, they will affect it nonetheless. For purposes of analysis, they may be placed into three categories: meeting the Soviet challenge, restraining the Congress, and straightening out the military pay system.

Meeting the Soviet Challenge

Although a consensus has developed that the military balance vis-à-vis the Soviet Union cannot be allowed to deteriorate further and that the Pentagon will be permitted to increase its budget in real terms for the foreseeable future, the Department of Defense has not developed a coherent set of policies on the most appropriate ways to use the additional funds to offset Soviet advances.[1] This lack of clear direction applies to the policies which will shape both our strategic and conventional forces.

Strategic Forces

The keystone of our strategic deterrent is a triad of land-based intercontinental ballistic missiles (ICBMs), submarine-launched ballistic missiles (SLBMs), and intercontinental manned bombers. The triad of 1,054 ICBMs, 656 SLBMs, and 400 bombers developed in the mid-1960s has remained essentially unchanged in number and capability over the past decade. However, because of Soviet advances and obsolescence, over the next ten years the Pentagon leadership will have to make some difficult choices about each leg of the triad. These decisions may well determine the viability of our strategic deterrent against the Soviets.

ICBM Forces

As of 1978, the Soviet Union had the capability to destroy about 50 percent of our land-based ICBM forces with a preemptive first strike. By 1983, increases in the number of warheads in the Soviet arsenal, coupled with improvement in their accuracy, will enable the Russians to destroy more than 90 percent of our silos by using only a fraction of their strategic rocket force.[2]

The United States has not yet decided how to cope with the threat to the only leg of the triad which offers a prompt, high-confidence, counterattack capability against a broad spectrum of both hard and soft targets. Instead, the Pentagon has worked spasmodically and often simultaneously on four distinctly different approaches, without settling on any one.

The first approach was to develop a new generation of ICBMs and make them mobile. In the early 1970s, DOD began work on an advanced ICBM—the MX-1 system. DOD wanted to build 300 of these missiles. To ensure survivability the MX was to have been placed in a ten- to twenty-mile-long trench system. A missile transporter-launcher was supposed to move at random intervals inside the trench, thus leaving the Soviets almost totally uncertain of the exact location of the missile along the length of the trench.[3] The original time frame called for beginning production of the MX in 1978 with actual deployment in 1984. In 1976, President Ford, alarmed by Soviet advances in strategic weaponry, accelerated the timetable. He wanted production to begin in 1977 and deployment by 1983. However, in 1977 and again in 1978, President Carter delayed the program so that the MX cannot begin deployment before 1986.

A second approach has been to develop a Multiple Aim Point (MAP) system for the entire ICBM force.[4] This plan, which was first formulated in late 1977, envisions digging up to twenty different holes or silos for each missile, and moving the missile at random intervals among the holes. Thus, if the Soviets wished to destroy the missile force on the ground they would have to target all twenty holes. Assuming that two warheads would be needed to destroy each missile, the Soviets would need about 40,000 warheads to destroy 1,000 Minuteman missiles and an additional 6,000 warheads to destroy 300 MX missiles. A third approach formulated in 1978 called for building the MX and placing it on a wide-bodied aircraft.

A fourth approach, developed in 1978, was the adoption of a launch on warning or launch strategy, that is, a policy of firing our missiles before the Soviet missiles actually impact upon our silos.[5] Adoption of this strategy requires improvement of our early warning and command and control systems, but does not necessitate the development of new missiles, trenches, or additional silos.

Each of these approaches has its strengths and weaknesses. Adopting a launch under attack option is comparatively inexpensive but potentially very destabilizing; it literally puts a hairtrigger on nuclear war. Placing the MX in a mobile mode in a trench system would be prohibitively expensive—about \$35 to \$40 billion, and fraught with technological problems. The MAP system would cost about half as much as the MX and would have fewer technological obstacles, but it could be quite destabilizing if it leads to pressures to place real missiles in those empty holes. Placing the new ICBM on an aircraft would increase survivability but would degrade accuracy and would require building new planes. However, time is running out and one of these options must be adopted soon if this program is to remain viable.

SLBM Forces

The SLBM portion is also experiencing problems. However, its difficulties arise not because it is becoming vulnerable but because the present force is becoming obsolete so rapidly that its replacements will not be ready on time.[6] Moreover, the next generation of fleet ballistic missile submarines is so costly that DOD may not be able to modernize the most secure leg of the triad.

Our present SLBM force is composed of ten submarines equipped with Polaris missiles and thirty-one submarines equipped with Poseidon missiles. The Polaris boats, Washington and Allen class submarines, were commissioned between December 1959 and January 1963 and designed to last twenty years. Thus, these ten boats should be replaced between December 1979 and January 1983.

The thirty-one Poseidon boats, Lafayette class submarines, were commissioned between April 1963 and April 1967. Originally, they too were designed to last twenty years and carry Polaris missiles. However, the modifications done to the Lafayette submarines in the early 1970s to enable them to carry the larger Poseidon missile make it possible to extend their lives to at least twenty-five and possibly thirty years. Ideally, the Poseidons should be replaced between 1983 and 1987 but, if necessary, they may be able to last until the following decade.

In the early 1970s the Pentagon began developing the Trident submarine as a follow-on. This submarine is enormous. It is 650 feet long, has an 18,700-ton displacement, and is powered by a 90,000-horsepower nuclear reactor. Originally, the Pentagon intended to build ten Tridents to replace the ten Polaris boats at a rate of three every two years, beginning in 1979. In 1974 and again in 1975, DOD officials tried to persuade Congress to approve a Narwahl class submarine as a replacement for the Poseidon fleet.[7] These men were not able to convince Congress that the Narwahl, which was smaller and cheaper than Trident, was a viable option. Therefore, between 1976 and 1978, the size of the Trident program was increased from ten to thirteen.[8]

However, during that same period, the Trident program encountered great difficulties. The lead boat fell two years behind schedule and production costs rose so rapidly that the program of funding three submarines every two years could not be maintained. This situation has confronted the Pentagon with a painful dilemma.

On the one hand, it can continue to rely exclusively on Trident as a replacement for both Polaris and Poseidon. Twenty-five Tridents would provide more than enough firepower to replace the present force of forty-one submarines.[9] However, this option would be prohibitively expensive, $35-$45 billion, and would result in a temporary shortfall as the older Polaris boats have to retire before the new Tridents are ready to come on line.

On the other hand, DOD can terminate the Trident program at thirteen boats and develop another smaller and less costly submarine. While this option would not solve the shortfall problem, it will probably be less expensive. However, it could lead to unforeseen technological and production problems that often befall new weapons systems. Whatever choice is made will also have to be made quickly and will have a profound impact upon the capabilities of what is at present the most secure leg of the triad.

Manned Bomber Forces

For the near term, DOD must rely on the B-52 to maintain the viability of the bomber leg of the triad. President Carter's June 1977 decision to halt B-1 production leaves the Pentagon no other choice. The Air Force intends to equip 150 B-52s with 3,000 cruise missiles and use them as standoff weapons. This program will commence in 1981. The other 150 B-52s will be maintained as penetrating bombers. For two reasons, the mixed force of B-52s must remain only a short-term solution to the bomber question.

First, the B-52s are simply wearing out. Most are older than the pilots flying them. The production line for these planes was closed in 1962. Most of the B-52s in the force were built in the 1950s and designed for a useful life of twenty years. Thus, even with modifications it will be difficult to extend the usefulness of these planes past the mid-1980s. Second, as Soviet air defenses become more sophisticated the B-52 is rapidly losing its penetration capabilities. Even now, the B-52, with a low altitude penetration height of 400 feet at a speed of Mach .53, does not pose an overwhelming threat to the massive Soviet strategic defensive system.[10] Thus, DOD soon will have to begin development of a new plane or planes designed to carry cruise missiles and penetrate Soviet air space if it wishes to maintain the viability of its bombers. The Air Force does not have another plane ready to go.

Essentially, the Pentagon has two options. First, it can design an entirely new plane, a BX, to perform both missions. This aircraft could not be ready to move into production before the late 1980s, and its cost would be at least $30 billion. Second, it can modify some wide body commercial or military aircraft to fulfill the cruise missile carrier (CMC) role and modify the FB-111A to serve as a penetrating bomber. (The modified version would be known as an FB-111H.) These planes could be operational in the mid-1980s at a cost of about $18 billion.

Both options have their strengths and weaknesses. The BX would be more capable but more costly and would not be ready on time. The CMC/FB-111 combination would be less expensive and more timely but not nearly as capable. The CMC would be extremely vulnerable to Soviet aircraft and missiles while the FB-111 has about the same penetrating capabilities as the B-52.[11] Whatever choice is made will have a profound effect on the oldest and most flexible leg of our strategic deterrent force.

Conventional Forces

The key question regarding conventional forces involves the emphasis DOD should place in structuring them. Basically, there are two schools of thought. The first is based on the assumption that the greatest threat to our security is a blitzkrieg attack by the Warsaw Pact forces in Europe. Therefore, our general purpose forces should be designed primarily to fight a short intensive war on the central front in Europe. This viewpoint assumes that, if our forces can handle that threat, they will necessarily be capable of handling lesser contingencies. The second viewpoint makes the assumption that since this nation has never been willing to pay the full cost of providing the forces necessary to support our policies, we ought to compensate for this shortcoming by developing flexible forces, that is, forces capable to being used in more than one place and for many purposes.

If the first plan is adopted then top priority within the additional funds available in the defense budget would be given to increasing the firepower and readiness of Army ground divisions and Air Force tactical aircraft which will bear the brunt of any blitzkrieg attack. Naval, Marine, and reserve forces are not given much priority in this scenario. Sea control is not vitally important because the war will have to be fought with the manpower and equipment already in Europe or capable of being airlifted there within a short period of time. Similarly, Marine troops are too lightly armed to be used on the central front, and amphibious landings on the flanks of NATO, that is, Norway and Turkey, will have only a marginal impact on the outcome. Finally, reserve forces cannot be mobilized quickly enough to become involved in the fighting.

The second viewpoint gives much higher priority to forces of the Navy and Marine Corps because these two services can be used in so many ways. Naval ships can provide military presence throughout the globe and aircraft launched from floating platforms can project United States military power virtually anywhere on earth. Similarly, the Marines can fight and be interjected quickly into jungles, deserts, and even the Arctic.

During the post-Vietnam period, the Nixon and Ford administrations opted for the latter emphasis. Ford used the real increases in the defense budget in the FY 1976-1978 period to build a wide spectrum of defense capabilities. The Carter administration wants to place the primary emphasis on the NATO scenario. Its initial defense budgets added funds for the Army and Air Force and took them from the Navy and Marine Corps.[12] The choice that is made will have a great impact on the defense of this nation and the peace of the world.

Restraining the Congress

Congress has overreacted to its former passive role vis-à-vis the Pentagon. Prior to 1968, the legislature was too willing to give the

Pentagon a blank check to conduct its operations. A decade later, Congress is at the point of suffocating the Pentagon with information demands, is strangling the capabilities of the defense managers to operate the military establishment, and is preventing the executive branch from establishing a consistent defense policy.

Congressmen now send more than one million written and telephoned inquiries into the Pentagon each year. They put defense witnesses through some three thousand hours of questioning before seventy-two committees annually. Moreover, the trends are still upward; that is, the demands for information are still growing by leaps and bounds.

The legislature has subdivided the defense budget into some several thousand line items and has placed so many restrictions on each separate account that program managers literally cannot transfer funds or overspend individual accounts without "an act of Congress." In addition, Congress adds so many appendages to the defense appropriations bills that defense officials have very little flexibility in managing the department. In recent years, Congress has told the Pentagon such things as how many workers to hire in Naval shipyards, what type of power plants to place on its ships, how often to test airplanes before moving into production, and to admit women to its service academies. Not only do these recommendations hinder flexibility, but they are usually poorly conceived and violate sound management procedures. For example, since Congress placed a limit on the number of shipyard personnel, the Navy had to ask its allotted number of personnel to work overtime at time and a half. This not only increased costs but raised the accident rate. A nuclear-powered Navy increases ship costs so much that within the level of funds appropriated for shipbuilding the Navy has experienced great difficulty in constructing a sufficient number of ships to carry out its assigned missions.

Congressional involvement in the weapons procurement process has also become overbearing. Presently, there are approximately four thousand congressionally mandated restrictions on contractors doing business with the Pentagon. In addition, in recent years Congress has practiced an extreme form of "stop and go" appropriations, refusing to give a final definitive decision on most major weapon systems. These congressional actions have had at least three undesirable side effects. First, many producers have withdrawn from the defense market, oftentimes leaving the military services with no source of supply and weakening our mobilization base. In August 1975, the Pentagon actually had to ask the Justice Department to file suit against the Newport News Shipbuilding Company to force the firm to build a vitally needed guided missile cruiser because Newport News is the only United States shipyard qualified to build nuclear-powered surface ships.[13] Second, there has been a high turnover among defense contractors resulting in many inefficiencies as new firms break into the defense business. Third, there has been a reluctance on the part of many defense contractors to install modern, more efficient, cost-cutting equipment, thus driving up the cost of producing weapons.

When the Department of Defense attempted to bring this problem to the attention of the Congress and the public in a study called "Profit 76," many congressmen denounced the effort as the capstone in a new series of handouts to favored companies in the military-industrial complex.[14] While such denunciations made good press, they did not deal with the problem of the declining mobilization base for defense created in part by congressional overcontrol.

Most serious have been the attempts by Congress to intrude too deeply in the national security policy-making process. While no one expects Congress to merely rubberstamp executive branch initiatives, the legislative branch is not equipped to preempt the executive in this area. For example, it takes the executive branch about two years to develop a defense budget. Throughout this process major policy issues generated by the budget requests of the military services are debated and discussed by representatives of the military services, the Joint Chiefs of Staff, the Office of the Secretary of Defense, the Office of Management and Budget, and the President himself. Normally, the final product is a carefully balanced package designed to support specific policies; it usually has the support of all the various factions. The legislative branch then has approximately six months to examine the budget. Rather than taking the President's request as a starting point, the congressional committees now prefer to go back to the original requests of the armed services and begin the process a second time. Because they lack the time, the expertise, the discipline, and the cohesion, these congressional committees cannot do it as well as the executive branch. Moreover, by spending their time doing the work of the executive branch, the legislators are not able to perform what should be their primary function, namely, a public discussion of the implications of the policies developed by the executive branch.

The problems which can be created by this congressional attempt to become too deeply involved in the policy-making process were exemplified by the way in which it handled the FY 1979 defense budget, the first budget formulated completely by the Carter administration. This budget set a new tone for our defense policy; it wanted to give overwhelming priority to building up our conventional forces to handle a short intensive war in central Europe. Rather than debating the implications of this profound change in strategy, Congress spent its time reviewing such issues as whether an aircraft carrier should be funded in FY 1979 or the following year, and whether this carrier should be conventionally (oil) or nuclear powered, and whether the United States should have a new mobile intermediate-range missile system in Europe or continue to rely on the Pershing missile. The Carter administration, on the basis of a National Security Council Study and two Department of the Navy studies, had decided that as part of its five-year shipbuilding program it would fund a new conventionally powered carrier in the FY 1980 budget, and that a judgment on a new mobile missile should be postponed until an interagency study of theater nuclear weapons was completed. Congress, relying on the judgment of some Navy and Air Force personnel, voted to fund a nuclear carrier in the FY 1979 budget and ordered development of the new mobile missile to begin in FY 1979.

In making these decisions, Congress did not provide any rationale for overruling the three Navy studies nor did it elaborate on how the new mobile missile would affect the question of tactical nuclear weapons in Europe. The congressional intrusion in the policy-making process during its examination of the FY 1979 defense budget so concerned President Carter that he felt it necessary to veto the FY 1979 Defense Authorization Bill. It remains to be seen whether this will mark the watershed of congressional intrusion.

Straightening Out the Military Pay System

A third problem area is the military compensation system. To put it bluntly, the entire compensation system is a mess. Retirement costs are eating up a larger and larger portion of the defense budget. By FY 1979, they had risen above $10 billion.

The retirement system was designed to operate in an environment where active duty military pay was comparatively low and inflation was modest. Neither of these conditions is applicable any longer. Since 1972, active duty compensation has been more than comparable to the prevailing wage structure in private industry or other departments of the federal government. As is indicated in Table 40, by 1975 regular military compensation had risen to more than 20 percent above its corresponding civilian level. Since 1968, inflation has averaged nearly 6 percent a year and, if anything, will be higher in the next decade. The military retirement system is so designed that each time the inflation rate exceeds 3 percent for three consecutive months, the retiree receives an automatic increase to cover the inflation. Thus, he has been getting two raises per year.

As far back as 1972 the Pentagon proposed legislation to amend its retirement system to reflect the new environment. However, the Retirement Modernization Act of 1972 has languished on Capitol Hill since that time, primarily because it has received only lukewarm support from the uniformed leaders of our armed services.

In 1974, Congress established the Defense Manpower Commission to study the system, and, in 1977, President Carter set up a Commission on Military Compensation. Both the congressional group and Carter's commission endorsed the essentials of the Retirement Modernization Act, that is, elimination of an immediate annuity of 50 percent upon completion of twenty years of service and an offset when the retiree begins to receive social security.[15] Nonetheless, the military leaders still will not support a change in the system.

The active duty compensation picture is not much brighter. When the pay and allowances of military personnel are added, their compensation level is quite high. However, the system is so "muddled," that is, the compensation comes in so many different forms and has so many variations even for people in the same grade,

Table 40   Selected Examples of Annual Compensation for Military and Civilian Personnel (pay scales as of October 1, 1975)

Pay Grade	Military Grade (Army Title)	LOS[2]	Number of Dependents	Basic Pay	Quarters	Subsistence	Federal Tax Advantage	RMC[1]	Salary[3]	Comparable Grade
O-10	General	26	1	$37,800	$3,830	$637	$3,627	$45,894		
O-9	Lieutenant General	26	2	37,800	3,830	637	3,541	45,808		
O-8	Major General	26	2	37,800	3,830	637	3,541	45,808	$37,800	GS-18
O-7	Brigadier General	26	2	33,142	3,434	637	3,043	40,652	38,800/37,800	GS-17/GS-16
O-6	Colonel	26	3	29,113	3,175	637	2,350	35,534	35,485	GS-15
O-5	Lieutenant Colonel	20	3	22,950	2,866	637	1,638	28,400	30,441/25,962	GS-14/GS-13
O-4	Major	14	3	18,522	2,599	637	1,234	23,258	21,970	GS-12
O-3	Captain	6	3	14,630	2,336	637	884	18,750	18,423/16,800	GS-11/GS-10
O-2	1st Lieutenant	2	2	10,058	1,883	637	675	13,707	15,278/13,850	GS-9/CS-8[4]
O-1	2nd Lieutenant	0	1	7,992	2,765	637	591	11,102	12,518	GS-7[4]
W-4	Chief Warrant Officer, W-4	26	3	18,371	2,549	637	1,188	22,960	[4]	
W-3	Chief Warrant Officer, W-3	20	3	14,501	2,311	637	856	18,542	[4]	
W-2	Chief Warrant Officer, W-2	16	3	12,218	2,138	637	641	15,807	[5]	
W-1	Warrant Officer, W-1	10	3	10,058	2,448	637	603	13,436	[5]	
E-9	Sergeant Major	22	3	14,350		923	905	18,626	11,274	GS-6

E-8	Master Sergeant	20	3	11,948	2,290	923	693	15,854	[6]
E-7	Sergeant, 1st class	18	3	10,404	2,146	923	667	14,140	[6]
E-6	Staff Sergeant	14	3	8,849	1,994	923	662	12,429	10,117 GS-9[7]
E-5	Sergeant	4	2	6,466	1,843	923	599	9,831	[7]
E-4	Corporal	2	1	5,512	1,613	923	537	8,585	9,040 GS-4
E-3	Private, 1st class	<2	0	5,018	961	923	467	7,370	8,050/7,136/6,299 GS-3/GS-2/GS-1[8]
E-2	Private	<2	0	4,831	850	923	433	7,037	
E-1	do	<2	0	4,334	799	923	406	6,464	

1. RMC is defined in law as basic pay, quarters and substance allowances (either in cash or in kind), and the federal tax advantage of those allowances. Cash rates were used for these examples. It must be recognized that many members, particularly in the lower enlisted grades, are required to live in government quarters and subsist in government dining facilities—e.g., barracks and ships—and do not receive cash allowances.

2. Average length of service for pay purposes of the personnel in each pay grade.

3. Pay rates for general schedule employees at the 5 of each pay guide.

4. GS-9/GS-8 comparable to military grades O-2, W-4, W-3.

5. GS-7 comparable to military grades O-1, W-2, W-1.

6. GS-6 comparable to E-9, E-8, E-7.

7. GS-5 comparable to E-6, E-5.

8. E-3, E-2, E-1 are comparable to GS-3, GS-2.

Source: *Armed Forces Journal*, January 1976, p. 10.

most members of the armed forces are unaware of how well paid they are. Moreover, many of the non-salary benefits are a carryover from the era when basic pay was quite low. Consequently, every time an attempt is made to control the burgeoning costs of military compensation by removing an outmoded benefit, the military men complain about "erosion of benefits," morale suffers, and reenlistment rates fall. In the area of compensation the Pentagon has to deal with the worst of all possible worlds, that is, high costs and a perception that benefits are low.

Although issues concerning military compensation are not nearly as stimulating as questions of strategy, tactics, or doctrine, they are no less important. If the military compensation system is not straightened out quickly, high personnel costs and disillusionment among the volunteer soldiers could make these questions moot. If active duty and retirement costs are not brought under control, there may not be sufficient funds to do anything meaningful about the triad or the NATO scenario. Similarly, without enough volunteers, the Pentagon will not have to worry about defending Central Europe or its flanks. It will not be able to do much about either.

Conclusion

These then are the major challenges facing the Pentagon and its leaders. If these problems are not handled as well as those of the post-Vietnam War era, disaster could befall the American military establishment, the American political system, and spaceship earth. The Department of Defense now stands at a precarious threshold. Through wise choices made by some exceptional leaders in a very difficult environment, it has overcome some extraordinary problems in the past decade. However, these advances may be jeopardized and the Pentagon could once again begin to "fall" if these new challenges are not met.

Notes

1. See, for example, the speech by Secretary of Defense Harold Brown to the Thirty-Fourth Annual Dinner of the National Security Industrial Association, Washington, D.C., September 15, 1977.

2. Harold Brown, *Annual Defense Department Report, FY 1979*, February 2, 1978, pp. 106-7, and Congressional Budget Office, *Counterforce Issues for U.S. Strategic Nuclear Forces*, January 1978, pp. 20-21.

3. For an excellent discussion of the MX see the following: "MX, A New Dimension in Strategic Deterrence," *Air Force Magazine*, September 1976, pp. 44-49; John Baker, "The MX ICBM Debate," *Arms Control Today*, February 1977, pp. 1-4.

4. For an excellent discussion of MAP by General Lew Allen, current Air Force Chief of Staff, see George Wilson, "Missile Hole Plan Seen as Cure to Soviet Buildup," *Washington Post*, July 13, 1978, p. 10.

5. Brown, *FY 1979 Defense Report*, p. 106.

6. Ibid., p. 111.

7. James Schlesinger, *Annual Defense Department Report, FY 1975*, March 4, 1974, p. 60.

8. Assistant Secretary of Defense (Comptroller), *Selected Acquisition Reports*, February 14, 1978.

9. Twenty-five Tridents would have 600 missiles equipped with 6,672 warheads. The present 41-boat force has 656 missiles and 5,120 warheads.

10. The Soviet strategic defensive system has more than 10,000 surface-to-air missile launchers, 6,500 air defense surveillance radars, and 2,600 interceptor aircraft.

11. Ronald Tammen, "The Bomber Debate: Is There a B-2 in Our Future," *Arms Control Today*, November 1977, p. 3.

12. See my *The FY 1979-1983 Defense Program: Issues and Trends* (Washington, D.C.: American Enterprise Institute, 1978), for an analysis of the Carter defense program.

13. Charles Corddry, "U.S. Going to Court over Navy Cruisers," *Baltimore Sun*, August 29, 1975, p. 6.

14. See, for example, the remarks of Senator William Proxmire (D-Wis.) in "Pentagon Seeking to Boost Profits," *Washington Star*, August 23, 1975, p. 3.

15. For an excellent summary of the reports of various groups on the subject of military retirement see *Report of the President's Commission on Military Compensation*, April 10, 1978, pp. 191-93.

Bibliography

Books

Aron, Raymond. *The Imperial Republic*. Cambridge, Mass.: Winthrop, 1974.

Art, Robert. *The TFX Decision*. Boston: Little, Brown, 1968.

Betts, Richard. *Soldiers, Statesmen and Cold War Crises*. Cambridge, Mass.: Harvard University Press, 1977.

Binkin, Martin. *The Military Pay Muddle*. Washington, D.C.: Brookings Institution, 1975.

———— *U.S. Reserve Forces*. Washington, D.C.: Brookings Institution, 1974.

Blechman, Barry, Gramlich, Edward, and Hartman, Robert. *Setting National Priorities, The 1976 Budget*. Washington, D.C.: Brookings Institution, 1975.

Bletz, Donald. *The Role of the Military Professional in U.S. Foreign Policy*. New York: Praeger, 1972.

Borklund, Carl. *Men of the Pentagon*. New York: Praeger, 1966.

Brown, Harold. *Annual Defense Department Report, FY 1979*. Washington, D.C., 1978.

Bunting, Josiah. *The Lionheads*. New York: G. Braziller, 1972.

Clotfelter, James. *The Military in American Politics*. New York: Harper and Row, 1973.

Congressional Quarterly. *The Power of the Pentagon*. Washington, D.C., 1972.

Department of Defense (Comptroller). *The Economics of Defense Spending: A Look at the Realities*. Washington, D.C., 1972.

Donovan, James. *Militarism U.S.A.* New York: Scribners, 1970.

Eisenhower, Dwight D. *Waging Peace*. Garden City, N.Y.: Doubleday, 1956.

Enthoven, Alain, and Smith, K. Wayne. *How Much Is Enough*. New York: Harper and Row, 1971.

Fox, T. Ronald. *Arming America: How the U.S. Buys Weapons*. Cambridge, Mass.: Harvard University Press, 1974.

Furgurson, Ernest. *Westmoreland: The Inevitable General*. Boston: Little, Brown, 1968.

Gabriel, Richard, and Savage, Paul. *Crisis in Command*. New York: Hill and Wang, 1978.

Halbestram, David. *The Best and the Brightest*. New York: Random House, 1972.

Halperin, Morton. *Bureaucratic Politics and Foreign Policy*. Washington, D.C.: Brookings Institution, 1974.

Hauser, William. *America's Army in Crisis*. Baltimore: Johns Hopkins, 1973.

Herbert, Anthony. *Soldier*. New York: Holt, Rhinehart and Winston, 1972.

Hilsman, Roger. *The Politics of Policy Making in Defense and Foreign Affairs*. New York: Harper and Row, 1971.

Hoopes, Townsend. *The Limits of Intervention*. New York: McKay, 1973.

Huntington, Samuel. *The Soldier and the State*. New York: Vintage, 1957.

Johnson, Lyndon. *The Vantage Point*. New York: Holt, Rhinehart and Winston, 1971.

Kalb, Marvin, and Kalb, Bernard. *Kissinger*. Boston: Little, Brown, 1974.

Kaufmann, William. *The McNamara Strategy*. New York: Harper and Row, 1964.

Kissinger, Henry. *American Foreign Policy*. New York: W. W. Norton, 1974.

Kolko, Gabriel. *The Roots of American Foreign Policy*. Boston: Beacon Press, 1969.

Kolodziej, Edward. *The Uncommon Defense and Congress*. Columbus: Ohio State University Press, 1966.

Korb, Lawrence. *The FY 1979-83 Defense Program*. Washington, D.C.: American Enterprise Institute, 1978.

_____. *The Joint Chiefs of Staff: The First Twenty Five Years*. Bloomington: Indiana University Press, 1976.

_____. *The System for Educating Military Officers in the U.S.* Pittsburgh: International Studies Association, 1975.

Laswell, Harold. *The Analysis of Political Behavior*. London: Anchor Books, 1966.

Liska, George. *Imperial America*. Baltimore: Johns Hopkins, 1974.

Loory, Stuart. *Defeated: Inside America's Military Machine*. New York: Random House, 1973.

Lovell, John, and Kronenberg, Philip. *New Civil Military Relations*. New Brunswick, N. J.: Transaction, 1974.

Lubell, Samuel. *The Hidden Crisis in American Politics*. New York: Norton, 1971.

Lucas, William. *The Organizational Politics of Defense*. Pittsburgh: International Studies Association, 1974.

Magdoff, Harry. *The Age of Imperialism: The Economics of United States Foreign Policy*. New York: Monthly Review Press, 1969.

Merrit, Richard. *Foreign Policy Analysis*. Boston: D. C. Heath, 1975.

Middleton, Drew. *Can America Win Another War?* New York: Scribners, 1975.

Mollenhoff, Clark. *The Pentagon: Politics, Profits and Plunder*. New York: Pinnacle Books, 1972.

Mondale, Walter. *The Accountability of Power*. New York: David McKay, 1976.

Murdock, Clark. *Defense Policy Formulation*. Albany: State University of New York Press, 1974.

Nixon, Richard. *The Memoirs of Richard Nixon*. New York: Grosset and Dunlap, 1978.

Ott, David. *Nixon-McGovern and the Federal Budget*. Washington, D.C.: American Enterprise Institute, 1972.

_____. *Public Claims on U.S. Output: Federal Budget Options in the Last Half of the Seventies*. Washington, D.C.: American Enterprise Institute, 1973.

Owen, Henry. *Setting National Priorities: The Next Ten Years.* Washington, D.C.: Brookings Institution, 1976.

Roherty, James. *Decisions of Robert S. McNamara.* Coral Gables, Fla.: University of Miami Press, 1970.

Rourke, Francis. *Bureaucracy and Foreign Policy.* Baltimore: Johns Hopkins, 1972.

Rumsfeld, Donald. *Annual Defense Department Report, FY 1978.* Washington, D.C., 1977.

Sanders, Ralph. *The Politics of Defense Analysis.* New York: Dunellen, 1973.

Sarkesian, Sam. *The Military Industrial Company: A Reassessment.* Beverly Hills: Sage, 1974.

Schlesinger, James. *Annual Defense Department Report, FY 1976.* Washington, D.C., 1975.

Schram, Martin. *Running for President 1976.* New York: Stein and Day, 1978.

Stein, Harold. *American-Civil Military Decisions.* Tuscaloosa: University of Alabama Press, 1963.

Stockfish, Jacob. *Plowshares into Swords.* New York: Manson and Lipscomb, 1973.

Taylor, Maxwell. *Swords and Plowshares.* New York: W. W. Norton, 1973.

————. *The Uncertain Trumpet.* New York: Harper, 1960.

Westmoreland, William. *A Soldier Reports.* New York: Doubleday, 1976.

Yarmolinsky, Adam. *The Military Establishment.* New York: Harper and Row, 1971.

Zumwalt, Elmo. *On Watch.* New York: Quadrangle, 1976.

Articles

Blechman, Barry, and Fried, Edward. "Controlling the Defense Budget." *Foreign Affairs*, January 1976, pp. 240-41.

Clifford, Clark. "A Vietnam Appraisal." *Foreign Affairs*, July 1969, pp. 601-22.

Davis, Vincent. "American Military Policy: Decision-Making in the Executive Branch." *Naval War College Review*, May 1970, pp. 4-23.

Dulles, John Foster. "Policy for Security and Peace." *Foreign Affairs,* April 1954, pp. 15-30.

George, Alexander. "The Case for Multiple Advocacy in Making Foreign Policy." *American Political Science Review*, September 1972, pp. 751-85.

Ginsburgh, Robert. "A New Look at Control of the Seas." *Strategic Review*, Winter 1976, pp. 86-89.

Grant, Zalin. "Revolt in the Pentagon." *New Republic*, October 4, 1969, pp. 17-20.

Greenwood, Ted, and Nacht, Michael. "The New Nuclear Debate: Sense or Nonsense?" *Foreign Affairs*, July 1974, pp. 761-80.

Halperin, Morton. "The President and the Military." *Foreign Affairs*, January 1972, pp. 310-24.

Holloway, James. "The Transition to V/STOL," *Naval Institute Proceedings*, September 1977, pp. 19-24.

Korb, Lawrence. "The Bicentennial Defense Budget: A Critical Appraisal." *Armed Forces and Society,* Fall 1975, pp. 128-39.

————. "The Defense Budget and Detente." *Naval War College Review*, Summer 1975, pp. 19-27.

————. "The Joint Chiefs of Staff: Access and Impact in Foreign Policy." *Policy Studies Journal*, December 1974, pp. 170-74.

————. "The Issues and Costs of the New United States Nuclear Policy." *Naval War College Review*, November-December 1974, pp. 28-41.

————. "Congressional Impact upon the Defense Budget: The Fiscal and Programmatic Hypotheses." *Naval War College Review*, November-December 1973, pp. 49-62.

————. "The Secretary of Defense and the Joint Chiefs of Staff: Conflict in the Budgetary Process." *Naval War College Review*, December 1971, pp. 21-42.

————. "Robert McNamara's Impact upon the Budget Strategies of the Joint Chiefs of Staff."*Aerospace Historian*, Winter 1970, pp. 132-36.

Leacocos, John. "Kissinger's Apparat." *Foreign Policy*, Winter 1971, pp. 21-30.

Leggett, Robert. "Two Legs Do Not a Centipede Make." *Armed Forces Journal*, February 1975, pp. 3-20.

Scoville, Herbert. "Flexible Madness." *Foreign Policy*, Spring 1974, pp. 164-77.

Shoup, David. "Our New American Militarism." *Atlantic*, April 1969, pp. 51-56.

Tammen, Ronald. "The Bomber Debate: Is There a B-2 in our Future." *Arms Control Today*, November 1977, pp. 1-4.

Taylor, Maxwell. "The Exposed Flank of National Security." *Orbis*, Winter 1975, pp. 1011-22.

————. "The Legitimate Claims of National Security." *Foreign Affairs,* April 1974, pp. 577-94.

Zuckert, Eugene. "The Service Secretary: Has He a Useful Role?" *Foreign Affairs*, April 1966, pp. 458-79.

Glossary

ABM	Antiballistic missile system
A-10	Low-cost attack aircraft being developed by the Air Force to support ground troops
B-52	Long-range strategic bomber built in the mid-1950s
B-1	Proposed follow-on to the B-52
CNO	Chief of Naval Operations, head of the Navy, and a member of the JCS
CVN	Nuclear-powered aircraft carrier
DD	Destroyer
DOD	Department of Defense
F-4	High-performance fighter aircraft built in the 1960s and used by the Navy and Air Force
F-14	High-performance fighter being developed by the Navy for defense of its aircraft carriers
F-15	High-performance fighter being developed by the Air Force
F-16	Low-cost fighter being developed for the United States and NATO Air Forces
F-18	Low-cost fighter being developed by the Navy to complement the F-14
FY	Fiscal Year
JCS	Joint Chiefs of Staff
JFM	Joint Force Memorandum, written by the JCS since 1969
JSOP	Joint Strategic Objectives Plan, composed by the JCS since the mid-1950s
MIRV	Multiple independently targeted re-entry vehicle, that is, placement of several warheads on a single missile
MPM	Major Program Memorandum, a document written by the OSD in the McNamara years
NSC	National Security Council
O and M	Operations and maintenance, a subsection of the defense budget
PEMA	Procurement of Equipment Missile Army, a budgetary line item

R and D   Research and development

R,D ,T,   Research, development, test, and evaluation, a budgetary
and E   category

Index

About the Author
Lawrence J. Korb is Professor of Management at the U.S. Naval War College in Newport, Rhode Island. His previous books include *The Joint Chiefs of Staff, The Price of Preparedness,* and *The System for Educating Military Officers.*